Cravings all togeth

CHRISSY TEIGEN

with ADEENA SUSSMAN

RECIPES TO LOVE

Clarkson Potter/Publishers | *New York*

All rights reserved. Published by Clarkson
Potter/Publishers, an imprint of Random
House, a division of Penguin Random
House LLC, New York.
www.clarksonpotter.com

CLARKSON POTTER is a trademark and
POTTER with colophon is a registered
trademark of Penguin Random House LLC.

Library of Congress record available at
lccn.loc.gov/2021024070; ebook record
available at lccn.loc.gov/2021024071

ISBN 978-0-593-13542-6
Ebook ISBN 978-0-593-13543-3
Special edition ISBN 978-0-593-23613-0

Printed in China

Photographer: Alex Lau
Food stylist: Tyna Hoang
Food stylist assistant: Scott Fletch
Prop stylist: Sophie Strangio
Prop stylist assistant: Jaclyn Kersheck
Photo shoot producer: 2D Creative Artists
Recipe testers: Paige Grandjean, Ian
Knauer, Renae Wilson

Editor: Francis Lam
Assistant editor: Lydia O'Brien
Art director and designer:
Stephanie Huntwork
Production editor: Mark McCauslin
Production manager:
Heather Williamson
Compositor: Merri Ann Morrell
Indexer: Elizabeth T. Parson

10 9 8 7 6 5 4 3 2 1

First Edition

FOR JACK

contents

intro~duction

Welcome to *Cravings Cookbook Season Three*! I am soooo happy to have you back (or joining us for the first time)! Since the birth of *Cravings*—which feels like 10,000 lifetimes ago—so much has happened: babies have come, career and life paths have zigzagged like wild tributaries. Not to mention the country itself, which has been through the RINGER. We've *all* been through the ringer. A nation divided, friends and families torn apart by fundamental differences. But there has been one constant: one thing has kept me sane, kept us happy, and kept us together—a damn good meal with the ones we care about.

Family (in whatever form that takes for each of us) is more important than ever, and we've gotten to see firsthand how crucial love is to our everyday existence. For far longer than anyone would have thought, human interactions were replaced with Zoom calls, and hugs became double-tapped hearts on Instagram. But mannnn, am I lucky that the act of creating a meal, whether it's for yourself or your people, is a passion for so many of you out there! Every day—Every. Single. Day.—you tag me on posts showing the world something you've cooked, and I see how you love to cook as much as I do, and it inspires me. You have no idea!

Look, I know what we write in books is supposed to be able to withstand the test of time, and hopefully by the time you read this, Covid is just a bad memory, but I'd be insane not to address the incredible, heartbreaking pandemic we have just been through. People have passed. People have suffered. There has been so much loss. We have all had to cope with this thing in one way or another, and many of us did it alone.

If there is any silver lining, during this time when we've been stuck inside, we've learned an incredible amount about ourselves and others, and we've learned about what we need and what and who we love. Whereas before we barreled ahead without pausing, now we're lucky to even *see* our people. Although impromptu dinner parties with friends have seemed like a relic of the past for so long, I also had a chance to realize that they will come back and we will appreciate them more than ever.

For over a year, I have found comfort in, well, comfort. "Comfort food" used to sound like a cliché, but those dishes and that idea have meant so much to me this past year. Cravings, by nature, are timely. They are urges. Moments. But comfort, hopefully, lasts. The recipes we have created for this book are meant to be a cookable arsenal to hold on to forever.

Without a doubt, I have just lived through a period more transformative than I could have ever imagined. We lived through personal trauma, with the loss of our unborn baby, Jack. And that turned a very private journey into personal love and acceptance of life and all of its wild, horrific, beautiful ups and downs. So many of you stood by us during that time! I cannot thank you enough. This journey changed me in ways nothing else ever could, and while it was the absolute most painful thing I have endured, I have emerged stronger and hungrier than ever. Hungry for my family, hungry for my friends, hungry for love, hungry for work, hungry to make you hungry, and just plain f*cking hungry.

And boy, did Adeena get to see that firsthand. Like in the past, she moved in with me to cook and write this book together . . . and if she thought she knew me before, phew, was she mistaken! Even I was wrong about me. I thought, "Hell, book three, how on earth am I gonna muster up a hundred more recipes without some kind of gimmick?" Do I do healthy? Quick-and-easy? Both? I couldn't think of a theme. All I knew was that I wanted to have color and JOY, to dive more into the veggie world, to maybe nottttt put ham and cheese into every recipe.

Then I realized that the biggest thing I've personally craved—and that I know we have *all* craved WORLDWIDE—is comfort. Finding joy and beauty in simplicity, in balance. Eating not just to nourish your body but also your soul. As always, we strive to keep our recipes interesting, keep them twisty, keep them Cravings. But some of the dishes here are a little bit simpler, a little bit more straightforward than ones you've seen from us in the past. And that's okay, because sometimes you just want something that tastes like the perfect version of something you've had a hundred times before. Because it just makes you feel like everything is going to be okay.

All these recipes were created by us but always, always, inspired by you. I hope these meals take you to your happy place, make your house even more of a home, and bring you all the cozy you're craving in these— or any—crazy times.

One Note Before You Start Cooking

There's only one thing you NEED to know before making these recipes. When I call for measured amount of kosher salt, use my one true love, Diamond Crystal. If you have Morton, decrease the amount by ⅓ to ½. Or if it's just an amount to taste . . . then just taste it!

breakfast

+ BRUNCH

john's perfect omelet

SERVES 1
ACTIVE TIME: 10 MINUTES
TOTAL TIME: 10 MINUTES

If I add them all up, I eat on average 4 to 6 eggs a day (Note to self: get a chicken???). Sometimes I do my Night Eggs—nothing more than a hard-boiled egg I season with salt and pepper—to keep myself full because I wake up starving in those pitch-black hours. Then there are Yai's Thai scrambled eggs with shallots, garlic, and bacon. And Adeena's Greenas with those perfect soft-boiled eggies.

But John, oh, John. John is our house eggspert (help me, the mom jokes cannot be stopped anymore), and this omelet is one of his masterpieces. Eggability is known to be the ultimate test of any great chef, and when you get it right, it's a beautiful thing and feels like such an accomplishment! And John always, always gets this right. The omelet is so thin that it is almost crepelike—it envelops the broccoli, onion, and cheese like wrapping paper over a gift. It's so flavorful and juicy, and that's even before I pour Cholula all over it.

3 eggs

Kosher salt and freshly ground black pepper

3 tablespoons olive oil

½ cup small broccoli florets

⅓ cup chopped onion

1 teaspoon minced garlic

1 slice American cheese

Cholula or other hot sauce

1 In a small bowl, beat the eggs and season lightly with salt and pepper. Heat 2 tablespoons of the oil in a nonstick 9-inch skillet over medium-high heat. Add the broccoli and onion, season generously with salt and pepper, and cook, stirring, for about 2 minutes, then add the garlic. Cook until the broccoli is tender-crisp and the onion begins to soften, another 2 minutes or so. Transfer to a plate.

2 Add the remaining tablespoon of oil to the skillet, reduce the heat to medium, then add the eggs and swirl to set slightly, 1 minute. Return the broccoli mixture to the skillet, arranging it in a 2-inch strip across the center of the omelet. Tear the cheese into bits and arrange it on top of the vegetables, then cook the omelet, tipping the pan gently now and then, until almost dry but with a few wet spots remaining, 2 to 3 minutes. Use a spatula to fold one side of the omelet over the broccoli center, then fold over the other side. Gently flip the omelet and slide it onto a plate. Season with salt and pepper and serve with hot sauce.

steak &
creamy
parmesan
eggs
on toast

SERVES 2
ACTIVE TIME: 30 MINUTES
TOTAL TIME: 30 MINUTES

Ohhhhh, how I brag about my creamy eggs—so creamy that people think they have cheese in them. But no, they don't, and just for the extremely skeptical, we even titled the original recipe for them "Cheesy but Cheeseless Creamy Eggs." Cooked lowwww and slowwww, they were made seven days a week in my house, and many of yours as well. I still make them all the time, and they just make the beginning of the day feel like magic.

But now . . . we have added glitter to the magic show—glitter in the form of cheese. Finely grated parmesan cheese. And then more glitter in the form of steak. Okay, the analogy is kind of falling apart, but whatever. When we made this recipe, it was truly a dish I kept giving back, bite after bite, saying, "No, okay, seriously, I'm done," until there was quite literally NOTHING left on the plate. If you want to make ABBBBBSOLUTELY SURE to find yourself in the same exact situation, use a thick slice of buttery brioche for the toast.

Steak

1 (12-ounce) New York strip steak (1¼ inches thick)

1 tablespoon vegetable oil

2 teaspoons chili powder

¾ teaspoon kosher salt

¼ teaspoon freshly ground black pepper

Eggs

6 eggs

2 tablespoons heavy cream

¼ teaspoon kosher salt

2 tablespoons unsalted butter

½ cup (1 ounce) finely grated Parmigiano-Reggiano cheese

2 thick (¾-inch) slices brioche or other white bread

Fresh cilantro leaves, for garnish

Hot sauce of your choice (It's always Cholula for me)

1 MAKE THE STEAK: Take the steak out of the fridge and let it sit at room temperature for 30 minutes; get your other ingredients ready in the meantime.

2 Rub the steak all over with the oil, then rub in the chili powder and season generously with salt and pepper. Heat a medium heavy-bottomed or cast-iron skillet over medium-high heat until very hot. Add the steak and cook until medium-rare (about 130°F if using a meat thermometer), 4 to 5 minutes per side.

3 WHILE THE STEAK IS COOKING, MAKE THE EGGS: Whisk the eggs in a medium bowl with the cream and salt. In a medium nonstick skillet, heat the butter over low heat, stirring occasionally, until the butter is melted but not super hot, 2 to 3 minutes. Add the eggs and cook, stirring constantly with a silicone spatula, until the eggs are custardy and form small curds, 12 to 14 minutes. Remove from the heat and stir in the cheese. Press some aluminum foil over the surface of the eggs to keep them warm.

4 While the eggs are still cooking (you'll be stirring while you cook the steak), remove the steak to a cutting board and let it rest for 10 minutes.

5. Toast the bread. After the resting time, cut the steak across the grain into thin slices. Top each toast slice with some steak and eggs. Garnish with the cilantro and serve with the hot sauce.

stuffed pb&j french toast with berry–browned butter sauce

MAKES 2 SANDWICHES
ACTIVE TIME: 15 MINUTES
TOTAL TIME: 25 MINUTES

Oooooooooohhhhh WEE, this recipe is BOMB. Now, of course, every recipe in this book excites me—that's why they're here! But this? As the kids say, we snapped. Your favorite peanut butter, scooped between two pillowy puffs of white bread, paired with bananas and drizzled with warrrrrrrm berry–browned butter sauce, dusted with powdered sugar . . . are you kidding me? Every bite is oozy heaven. I highly recommend making this on a lazy Sunday, as it WILL put you into a sleepytime food coma, drooly smiles included.

John and I always make one to share . . . then another to share. The math here says we should just make two to begin with.

7 tablespoons unsalted butter, plus more for topping the French toast

⅓ cup raspberry or blackberry jam or fruit preserves (we like St. Dalfour or Bonne Maman)

Kosher salt

6 tablespoons chunky peanut butter (not salt-free)

4 (½-inch-thick) slices brioche

1 medium banana, peeled and sliced into 12 rounds

2 eggs

3 tablespoons whole milk

1 teaspoon vanilla extract

5 teaspoons granulated sugar

Confectioners' sugar, for dusting

1 In a small saucepan, melt 2 tablespoons of the butter over medium heat until foamy and a few browned bits appear, 4 to 5 minutes. Stir in the jam, add 2 pinches of salt, and cook until the jam bubbles, 1 minute. Remove from the heat and cover to keep warm.

2 Spread 2½ tablespoons of the peanut butter on 2 slices of bread (5 tablespoons total), then arrange 6 of the banana slices on top of the peanut butter on each slice, leaving a little room around the edges if you can. Use another ½ tablespoon peanut butter on each of the 2 remaining slices of bread to spread a ½-inch border around the edges of the bread. Press them, peanut-buttered side down, onto the banana-topped slices, pressing to adhere a bit at the edges.

3 In a pie plate or shallow baking dish, whisk together the eggs, milk, vanilla, 1 teaspoon sugar, and 2 pinches of salt. Dip each sandwich in the egg mixture, letting it soak for 30 seconds before flipping carefully and letting the other side soak for 30 seconds. Transfer the sandwiches to a plate. Heat 3 tablespoons butter over medium heat in a 9- or 10-inch nonstick skillet until foamy.

4 Sprinkle the top of each sandwich with 1 teaspoon sugar, then carefully invert and arrange both sandwiches, sugared sides down, in the skillet and cook until golden brown and a bit darker in spots, 2 to 3 minutes. Sprinkle the uncooked side of each sandwich with 1 teaspoon sugar, then remove the sandwiches to a plate, wipe out the skillet, and add 2 more tablespoons butter.

5 Return the sandwiches, uncooked sides down, to the skillet and cook until the undersides are golden, 2 to 3 minutes. Arrange each sandwich on a plate, sprinkle with a touch of salt, add a pat of butter, dust with confectioners' sugar, and drizzle half the warm jam sauce over each sandwich.

pickly perfect
break-fast burgers

MAKES 4 BURGERS
ACTIVE TIME: 25 MINUTES
TOTAL TIME: 30 MINUTES

NOT that I am a competitive person, but ever since my first cookbook, I have felt that I needed to figure out how to top John's breakfast sandwich. As your classic overachiever, *he* made his own sage-scented sausage patties with an oozy egg on top and was quite pleased with himself.

So, at some point, I figured, what's better than a breakfast sandwich? A breakfast burger! A little salty pickle crunch, some raw-ish onion for sharpness, a juicy tomato, melty American, smoky Canadian bacon (an under-the-radar sleeper hit, like many things Canadian), and the breakfast touch: a thin, folded ommie on top. No, not everyone thinks burgers are for breakfast, but breakfast can be at 4 a.m., or 11:59. Don't take this win away from me! For this round: Teigen 1, Legend 0.

4 English muffins

5 tablespoons unsalted butter

¾ pound ground beef

¼ cup minced garlic-dill pickles

3 tablespoons minced white onion

1½ teaspoons Cholula hot sauce, plus more for serving

1 teaspoon kosher salt, plus more for seasoning

1 teaspoon garlic powder

Freshly ground black pepper

1 tablespoon vegetable oil

4 slices Canadian bacon

4 slices American cheese

4 eggs, lightly beaten

4 slices of ripe beefsteak tomato

4 tablespoons Kewpie or regular mayonnaise (see Note)

1 Split and toast the English muffins and brush each side of the muffins with ½ tablespoon butter. If you want, keep the muffins warm in a low oven or toaster oven.

2 In a mixing bowl, gently combine the beef, pickles, onion, hot sauce, 1 teaspoon salt, the garlic powder, and ground pepper in a bowl, incorporating well (but don't overmix). Form the meat mixture into 4 equal 4-inch patties about ½ inch thick.

3 Heat a large cast-iron skillet over medium-high heat. Add half the oil, then add the Canadian bacon and cook until lightly crisped, 1 to 2 minutes per side. Transfer to a plate and cover with foil to keep warm. Heat the remaining ½ tablespoon oil. Season both sides of the burgers with salt and pepper, and when the oil is shimmering hot, sear the burgers until the underside is charred and crisp, 3 minutes. Flip the burgers, lay a cheese slice on top of each burger, and cook an additional 3 minutes.

The Greatest Mayo

Blended with only egg yolks, seasoned with MSG, and hailing from Japan, Kewpie is like mayo on steroids: rich, umamilicious, and worth the couple of extra dollars.

4 While the burgers are cooking, heat an omelet pan or an 8- or 9-inch nonstick skillet over medium heat. Brush with ½ tablespoon butter, then pour half the beaten eggs (just under ½ cup) into the skillet and swirl to form an omelet. Lower the heat to medium-low and cook until the top is still shiny and just barely wet, 2 to 3 minutes. Carefully flip the omelet, cook 30 seconds, and slide onto a plate. Repeat with another ½ tablespoon butter and the rest of the beaten eggs. Fold each omelet round in half and fold again into a shape that will fit onto the sandwich.

5 Sprinkle the muffins with salt, then layer on the cheese-topped burgers, omelets, Canadian bacon, and tomato slices, spreading 1 tablespoon mayo on top of each tomato slice and seasoning each layer with salt and pepper. If some of the ingredients have cooled a bit, you can microwave the sandwiches, loosely topped with a clean kitchen towel or paper towel, for 30 to 45 seconds.

turkey, mushroom & pepperoncini tater tot hot dish

SERVES 6 TO 8
ACTIVE TIME: 20 MINUTES
TOTAL TIME: 1 HOUR 10 MINUTES

To the people of Minnesota, the correct way to make hot dish is a serious business. I have faced multiple side-eyes for playing fast and loose with it sometimes. A few things we can agree on: Hot dish always consists of frozen tater tots, creamy condensed canned soup, cheese, onions, and maybe sausage or bacon. (But if you use sausage, f*ck everyone who uses bacon, and vice versa.) You gotta appreciate the passion, but at the end of the day it is tater tots, cheese, and creamy soup. To me, ours is delicious, but I also have an open mind and I believe in doing it the way you want to do it. We know this one is good because we gathered around it and destroyed it in 48 seconds flat. If we can ever go outside again this will be one of those things you take to a family brunch, one that will knock you out so you don't have to hang out with that annoying uncle for the rest of the afternoon. Oh, and it serves approximately one-point-six thousand people. Make it your own, make it your way.

2 tablespoons vegetable oil, plus more for the skillet

1 small yellow onion, diced

3 to 4 garlic cloves, minced

1 pound ground turkey

8 ounces fresh cremini or button mushrooms, sliced (2½ cups)

½ teaspoon kosher salt

¼ teaspoon freshly ground black pepper

1 (10 ½-ounce) can cream of celery soup

¾ cup whole milk

½ cup jarred sliced pickled pepperoncini peppers, chopped

1½ cups (6 ounces) shredded sharp cheddar cheese

1½ pounds (about 5½ cups) frozen tater tots

Hot sauce, for serving

1 Preheat the oven to 425°F.

2 Heat the oil in a large (at least 4-quart) pot over medium heat. Add the onion and cook, stirring occasionally, until lightly golden, 9 to 10 minutes. Add the garlic and cook, stirring, 1 minute. Add the turkey, mushrooms, salt, and pepper and cook, stirring occasionally and breaking up the turkey with a wooden spoon, until the turkey is no longer pink, 5 to 6 minutes. Add the soup, milk, pepperoncini, and ½ cup (2 ounces) of the cheese. Stir until well combined.

3 Grease the bottom and sides of a heavy 10-inch high-sided skillet or baking dish with oil. Pour the filling into the skillet, then sprinkle the remaining 1 cup cheese evenly over the top. Starting from the outside of the skillet, arrange the tater tots until the entire top is covered, reserving any remaining tater tots for another use.

4 Place the skillet on a rimmed baking sheet and bake until the filling bubbles and the tater tots are crispy and light golden brown, 30 minutes. Turn the heat up to 475°F and bake until the tater tots are fully golden brown, another 10 to 15 minutes. Let stand 10 minutes before serving. Serve with hot sauce.

two-berry muffins
with hbo crumble

MAKES 12 MUFFINS
ACTIVE TIME: 20 MINUTES
TOTAL TIME: 55 MINUTES

I HATE continental breakfasts. On every continent. What the hell are they? They're lazy!!! Breakfast means eggs, you freaks. I think my anger toward them is rooted in the fact my dad used to practically live at Courtyard Marriotts and there is NOTHING a Courtyard Marriott loves more than bragging about their stale muffins and their airport-security-conveyor-belt bagel warmers. My god, the drama. Just get a f*cking toaster for f*ck's sake!! Anyhoo, let's just say I don't like a lot of muffins.

ADEENA

I think you started this headnote and it trailed off . . . anything else to say?

CHRISSY

LOL—what if I *was* done?

Muffins

1¾ cups flour

1¾ teaspoons baking powder

½ teaspoon ground cinnamon

¼ teaspoon ground nutmeg

¼ teaspoon fine sea salt

⅓ cup sour cream

2 tablespoons whole milk

1½ teaspoons vanilla extract

⅔ cup granulated sugar

¼ cup (packed) light brown sugar

5 tablespoons unsalted butter, at room temperature

2 eggs

½ cup white chocolate chips

1 cup fresh raspberries

¾ cup sliced fresh strawberries

½ cup mini marshmallows

HBO Crumble

1 cup Honey Bunches of Oats cereal

2 tablespoons unsalted butter, melted

2 tablespoons light brown sugar

⅛ teaspoon fine sea salt

1 Preheat the oven to 375°F. Line a 12-cup muffin tin with a double layer of cupcake liners.

2 MAKE THE MUFFIN BATTER: In a medium bowl, whisk together the flour, baking powder, cinnamon, nutmeg, and salt. In a separate, small bowl, whisk together the sour cream, milk, and vanilla until smooth.

3 In the bowl of a stand mixer fitted with the paddle attachment, combine the sugars and butter and beat on medium-high speed until fluffy, scraping down the sides of the bowl once or twice, 2 to 3 minutes.

4 Add the eggs and beat until fluffy, scraping down the sides of the bowl if necessary, 1 minute. Reduce the mixer speed to low and alternately add the flour and milk mixtures in 2 batches each, beating just until combined after each addition. Add the chocolate chips and beat on low speed until just combined, 10 seconds. Fold in ½ cup of the raspberries and the sliced strawberries by hand just until incorporated. Divide the batter evenly among the lined muffin cups (about ⅓ cup each). Press about 5 marshmallows and 1 or 2 raspberries into the top of each muffin.

5 MAKE THE HBO CRUMBLE: In a medium bowl, combine the cereal, butter, brown sugar, and salt and toss until everything is coated in butter. Top the batter in each muffin cup with about 1½ tablespoons of the crumble, pressing gently to adhere.

6 Bake the muffins until the tops are golden and a toothpick inserted into the center comes out clean, about 25 minutes. Cool the muffins in the tin on a wire rack for 10 minutes. Remove the muffins from the tin and serve warm or let cool completely.

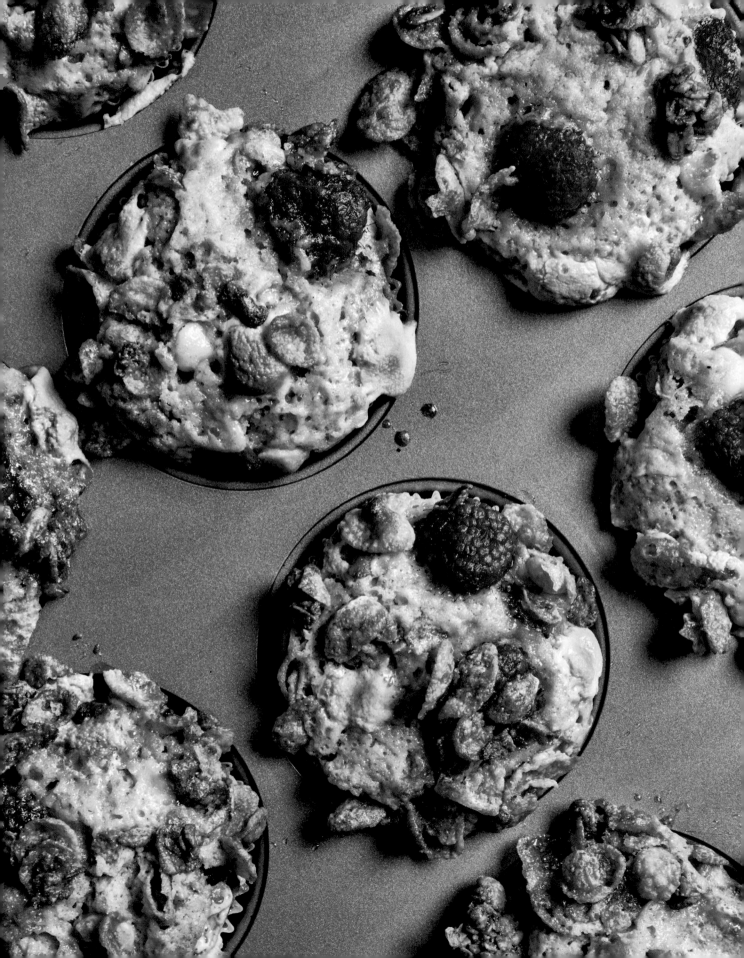

john's perfect blueberry buttermilk pancakes

MAKES 5 PANCAKES
ACTIVE TIME: 15 MINUTES
TOTAL TIME: 25 MINUTES

JOHN: These pancakes are *not* fancy. What they *are* is perfect. Fluffy, sweet, comforting, and so simple to make.

True, Chrissy actually already gave you some fancy-restaurant-brunch-worthy blueberry pancakes with "cream cheese bombs" in *Cravings 2*. Those go great with your mimosas and your beautiful, bougie friends. Mine is the recipe for family when they just want amazing pancakes and they're in pajamas and bathrobes. This recipe is what I make for our kids for our weekly tradition, "Pancake Sunday," at 7 a.m. Note that the recipe can be doubled.

A couple of quick notes: First, DON'T OVERSTIR! Leave your batter thick and a little lumpy; that's how it comes out so fluffy. Also, pick your syrup according to your own taste. Chrissy does NOT like fancy maple syrups. She prefers the one named after the Aunt who shall no longer be named. Choose wisely and enjoy!

1 cup flour

2 tablespoons sugar

1 teaspoon baking powder

½ teaspoon baking soda

½ teaspoon kosher salt

1 cup buttermilk, shaken

1 egg

2 tablespoons unsalted butter, melted and slightly cooled

Salted butter, straight from the stick

½ cup fresh blueberries (or ⅔ cup frozen blueberries, defrosted)

Maple syrup

1 Whisk the flour, sugar, baking powder, baking soda, and salt in a medium bowl. In another bowl, whisk together the buttermilk, egg, and 2 tablespoons butter until blended. Add the wet ingredients to the dry and stir until the dry is just incorporated; there should be no dry flour spots, but the batter will be lumpy and thick (that is the way it is supposed to be!).

2 Preheat a griddle over medium-low heat for a couple of minutes. Generously rub the griddle with salted butter and heat until it's foamy.

3 Use a ⅓-cup measure to ladle the pancake batter onto the griddle, as many as will fit comfortably. Scatter about 10 blueberries on the top of each pancake and cook until bubbles poke through the pancakes and the edges start to get a little lacy and brown, about 3 minutes.

4 Flip the pancakes, and while the underside is cooking, generously coat the browned tops of the pancakes with some salted butter. When the pancakes are finished (another 2 to 2½ minutes), transfer them to a plate. Wipe the griddle clean and repeat with fresh butter and the remaining batter. Top with more butter, if desired, and drizzle with maple syrup.

quiche lorraine
baguette

SERVES 4 AS A MAIN COURSE AND 8 AS AN APPETIZER
ACTIVE TIME: 30 MINUTES
TOTAL TIME: 1 HOUR 10 MINUTES

Imagine being the person to discover Ariana Grande. THAT'S what it felt like coming up with this classic.

I love quiche Lorraine—the egg custard, the melty gruyère cheese, the spinach, the mushrooms, the ham. I usually just pour the filling into a frozen pie crust and bake—but I am never *totally* satisfied. But then, every once in a while, the perfect recipe just slides into your imagination DMs and you know it's destiny. I started hollowing out a baguette, and I knew this was going to be a winner—I just felt it in my bones.

Soon I was posting about this long quiche in which the bread replaces the pie crust, and people flooded me with reactions like, "Oh, my god, WHAT is this? I MUST have this!" Slicing into it and hearing that crunch just sealed the deal. It holds together while still being moist and fluffy, and it's so full of flavor.

Bread choice is important here, so look for a baguette or a loaf with a firm outer crust (a little wider and shorter is even better than longer and skinnier). I plan on wrapping this up in foil, throwing it into my tote bag, and whipping it out at a brunch. It's beautiful, it's f*cking delicious, it's a forever recipe!

1 tablespoon unsalted butter

1 tablespoon olive oil

1 small onion, sliced

3 garlic cloves, minced

1¼ cups (4 ounces) sliced fresh mushrooms

1 teaspoon kosher salt, plus more for seasoning

½ teaspoon freshly ground black pepper, plus more for seasoning

5 eggs

¼ cup heavy cream

1 teaspoon Dijon mustard

5 slices deli ham

½ (10-ounce) package frozen spinach, defrosted and squeezed of excess liquid

½ cup (2 ounces) shredded gruyère or Swiss cheese

½ cup (2 ounces) shredded cheddar cheese

1 baguette (4 ×16-inch or 3 × 18-inch)

1 Preheat the oven to 375°F. Line a large baking sheet with aluminum foil.

2 Heat the butter and olive oil in a medium skillet over medium heat. Add the onion and cook, stirring, until partly softened, adding the garlic during the last minute, about 5 minutes total. Add the mushrooms, raise the heat to medium-high, and cook, stirring, until the mushrooms release their water and dry out, about 5 minutes. Season with salt and pepper and transfer to a plate.

3 In a medium bowl, whisk together the eggs, cream, mustard, and salt and pepper to taste. Dice 3 slices of the ham and fold that into the egg mixture along with the spinach, gruyère, cheddar, the cooled onion-mushroom mixture, 1 teaspoon salt, and ½ teaspoon pepper.

4 Use a serrated knife to make a 1½-inch-deep cut down the length of the baguette, stopping as the baguette tapers at the end. Use your hands to open the bread and hollow out the inside, leaving about ½ inch of bread along the sides and ¼ inch on the bottom. Use some aluminum foil to make a "boat," surrounding the bottom and outer sides of the baguette in case any filling tries to get out.

5 Carefully pack the baguette with the filling, opening it wider in the center to let the filling spread. Halve the remaining 2 pieces of ham and arrange them on top. Place the baguette on the baking sheet and bake until the egg is just set in the center, 35 to 40 minutes. Let cool for 2 or 3 minutes, then cut with a serrated knife.

snack + dips

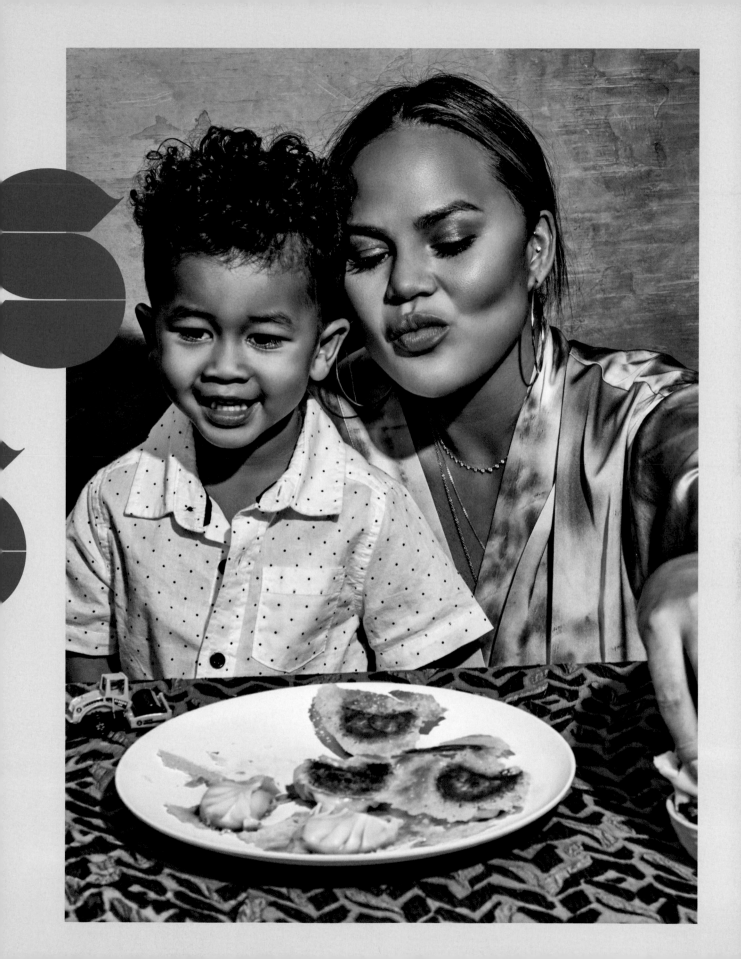

john's "tresa-dillas"

JOHN: I love making quesadillas for Chrissy. They're buttery, crispy, savory, and of course, very cheesy. I think of them as a grilled cheese sandwich with a thinner, flakier exterior. They're pretty quick and easy, and you can serve them as a late-night snack, as finger food at a party, or as lunch for the kids.

You can definitely just make a version with cheese and tortillas (I know you don't need a recipe for that), but I've taken some liberties. This is a cookbook, and we're going to get creative! Here are three combinations that are guaranteed to please—or take them in your own direction.

The rules for making your own quesadillas are simple. (1) Make sure the filling is full of flavor. (2) Make sure you don't skimp on the salted butter when you're frying. (3) Most important, fry them to a nice, crispy medium brown, for perfect appearance and taste.

RECIPE CONTINUES

smoky spinach, mushroom & cheddar

ACTIVE TIME: 35 MINUTES
TOTAL TIME: 35 MINUTES

Here's our veggie option, but this may be the best one I've ever made. It's garlicky and savory, plus sharp cheddar always feels like home to me because it reminds me of my mom's baked mac & cheese.

3 tablespoons olive oil

1 medium yellow onion, thinly sliced

½ (10-ounce) package fresh mushrooms, stemmed, cleaned, and thinly sliced

Kosher salt and freshly ground black pepper

½ (10-ounce) package frozen chopped spinach, defrosted and squeezed of excess liquid

½ teaspoon smoked paprika

Salted butter

2 large (8- or 9-inch) flour tortillas

¾ cup (3 ounces) grated sharp cheddar cheese

1 Heat a medium skillet over medium-high heat. Add 2 tablespoons of the olive oil, then add the onion and cook, stirring, until lightly golden, 9 to 10 minutes. Transfer to a plate.

2 Add the remaining tablespoon olive oil to the skillet, then add the mushrooms, season with salt and pepper, and cook, stirring, until they release their water and turn a little golden on the bottom, 4 to 5 minutes. Crumble the spinach with your hands and add it to the skillet along with the smoked paprika; cook until hot, 1 minute more. Transfer the mixture to a plate.

3 Run the skillet under cold water to clean it, then wipe dry with a paper towel.

4 Return the skillet to medium heat, then coat generously with butter. Add a tortilla to the skillet, then sprinkle half the cheese all over. Spread the mushroom mixture on it, then sprinkle on the remaining cheese. Top with the other tortilla and cook until the tortilla underneath shrinks and the edges appear golden, 3 to 4 minutes.

5 Slide the quesadilla onto a plate, then wipe the skillet out with a clean paper towel. Return the skillet to medium heat, coat generously again with butter, and flip the quesadilla back into the skillet to brown the other tortilla, another 3 minutes. Transfer to a cutting board and serve hot!

chorizo & pepper jack

ACTIVE TIME: 20 MINUTES
TOTAL TIME: 20 MINUTES

This one is meaty, with a spicy kick. The tomato was a last-minute idea that added a bit of fresh juiciness and turned out to be pretty clutch in making this come together as beautifully as it does.

½ pound loose chorizo sausage (or two 4-ounce links, casings removed)

Salted butter

2 large (8- or 9-inch) flour tortillas

¾ cup (3 ounces) grated pepper jack cheese

Handful of fresh cilantro leaves

3 or 4 slices of ripe tomato

Kosher salt

1 Heat a medium skillet over medium-high heat. Add the chorizo and cook, breaking up with a wooden spoon, until the chorizo releases its oil and is browned and cooked through, 6 to 7 minutes. Transfer to a plate, then drain any oil and juices left in the pan into a bowl.

2 Run the skillet under cold water to clean it, then wipe dry with a paper towel.

3 Return the skillet to medium heat, then coat generously with butter. Add a tortilla to the skillet, then sprinkle on half the cheese. Scatter the chorizo, then the cilantro and tomato slices. Season the tomato to taste with salt, then top with the remaining cheese and cover with the other tortilla. Cook until the bottom tortilla underneath shrinks and the edges appear golden, 3 to 4 minutes.

4 Slide the quesadilla onto a plate, then wipe the skillet out with a clean paper towel. Return the skillet to medium heat, coat generously again with butter, and flip the quesadilla back into the skillet to brown the other tortilla, another 3 minutes. Transfer to a cutting board and serve hot.

AVOCADO RANCH DIP
MAKES ABOUT 1 CUP

1 large avocado, ripe

⅔ cup buttermilk ranch dressing

1 large garlic clove, minced

1 teaspoon fresh lime juice

¼ teaspoon kosher salt

Mix the avocado, dressing, garlic, lime juice, and salt in a blender or food processor until smooth.

smoky chicken, bell pepper & swiss

WITH AVOCADO RANCH DIP

ACTIVE TIME: 25 MINUTES
TOTAL TIME: 1 HOUR 25 MINUTES
(INCLUDING MINIMUM MARINATING TIME)

Okay, maybe this will take a little more time because you have to sear some fresh chicken thighs. But it's very classy, and the ranch avocado dip is so dope. In fact, use this dip for any of these quesadillas because it'll taste great with just about anything.

2 skinless boneless chicken thighs (8 ounces total)

2 tablespoons olive oil

1 large garlic clove, finely minced

½ teaspoon smoked paprika

Kosher salt and freshly ground black pepper

½ medium green bell pepper, sliced

Salted butter

2 large (8- or 9-inch) flour tortillas

¾ cup (3 ounces) grated Swiss cheese

Avocado Ranch Dip (recipe at left)

Finely diced red onion and fresh cilantro leaves, for garnish

1 In a bowl, combine the chicken with 1 tablespoon of the olive oil, the garlic, smoked paprika, salt, and pepper. Marinate on the counter for up to 1 hour, or in the fridge for up to 24 hours.

2 Heat a medium skillet over medium-high heat. Add the thighs in one layer and cook until golden and juicy, 4 minutes per side. Transfer to a plate, leaving the juices and fat in the skillet. Add the bell pepper and cook until lightly charred and softened, 3 to 4 minutes. Transfer to a plate.

3 Run the skillet under cold water to clean it, then wipe dry with a paper towel.

4 Return the skillet to medium heat, then coat generously with butter. Add a tortilla to the skillet, then spread half the cheese on the tortilla, followed by the chicken, bell pepper, and remaining cheese. Top with the other tortilla and cook until the tortilla underneath shrinks and the edges appear golden, 3 to 4 minutes.

5 Slide the quesadilla onto a plate, then wipe the skillet out with a clean paper towel. Return the skillet to the heat, coat generously again with butter, and flip the quesadilla back into the skillet to brown the other tortilla, another 3 minutes. Transfer to a cutting board and serve with the Avocado Ranch Dip and a sprinkling of red onion and cilantro.

spicy crab dip

with chile-butter toasts

SERVES 10 TO 12
ACTIVE TIME: 15 MINUTES
TOTAL TIME: 40 MINUTES

Speaking as someone who currently has the remnants of this stuff in the corners of her mouth, allow me to AVIDLY vouch for this crab dip as the best damn crab dip you will EVER enjoy. I mean, I know writing cookbooks pretty much means bragging about how everything *you* make is theeeeee single way everyone should make things, but that really goes for this crab dip.

Now, while many crab dips hold the trinity key (is that a thing?) that is cream cheese, sour cream, and mayo, I don't think you'll find too many using the umami bomb that is fish sauce (bye-bye, worchestershirshirchesworshire).

Jumbo lump crab can be damn expensive, but if you can find it at a reasonable price or even use imitation, I have no problem saying that this is a dip worth taking home to your friends in Maryland. And I don't say that often. Trust me.

Dip

1 (8-ounce) package cream cheese, at room temperature

½ cup mayonnaise

3 tablespoons sour cream

1 cup (4 ounces) shredded sharp cheddar cheese

½ cup (1 ounce) finely grated Parmigiano-Reggiano cheese

1 tablespoon hot sauce (preferably Cholula, my fave)

2 teaspoons Old Bay seasoning

½ to 1 teaspoon fish sauce, depending on how salty you like things

1 scallion (white and green parts), thinly sliced, plus greens for garnish

1 pound lump crabmeat (the bigger the lumps the pricier, so just get what works for you!), drained if necessary

Topping

2 tablespoons unsalted butter

1 teaspoon Old Bay seasoning

30 Ritz crackers (1 sleeve)

2 tablespoons finely grated Parmigiano-Reggiano cheese

Toasts

½ small baguette

3 tablespoons unsalted butter, melted

1 tablespoon hot sauce (again, Cholula)

1 MAKE THE DIP: Arrange a rack in the top third of the oven. Preheat the oven to 350°F. In a large bowl, stir together the cream cheese, mayo, sour cream, and cheeses until smooth. Now stir in the hot sauce, Old Bay, fish sauce, and sliced scallion until incorporated. Then stir in the crab (the more you stir, the more broken up the crab will be). Spread the dip in an ovenproof 8-inch square dish (glass, ceramic, metal—all work).

2 MAKE THE TOPPING AND BAKE THE DIP: Melt the butter in a small bowl in the microwave in 30-second zaps until just melted. In a medium bowl, combine the melted butter with the Old Bay. Crush the crackers straight into the bowl, leaving some bigger pieces. Add the cheese and toss to blend. Top the dip with the cracker mix and bake until the top is golden and toasty, 18 to 20 minutes.

3 MAKE THE TOASTS: When the dip comes out of the oven, preheat the broiler. Cut the baguette into ¼-inch-thick slices and arrange on a baking sheet. In a small bowl, combine the butter and hot sauce and brush the toasts with the spicy butter. Broil until golden and the edges are dark. Serve with the dip, garnished with scallion greens.

bali-inspired chicken satay

SERVES 6 AS AN APPETIZER OR 3 AS A MAIN
ACTIVE TIME: 40 MINUTES
TOTAL TIME: 1 HOUR 10 MINUTES (INCLUDING CHILLING TIME)

I feel like I never stop talking about my trips to Bali, but when you love something . . . you just can't shut up about it. Twice we've gone there after I've had a baby, and it's a place where I am just so happy to be with our family, in a healthy, calm mindset. We always do cooking classes there, and the place we stay created the most gorgeous cookbook, *The Pleasures of Eating Well*. Every time before a class, I flip through its pages to find the bright, beautiful, natural, healthy, satisfying things I want to make. This satay was the first, and it will always be my favorite. When you bring it up to your mouth, it infuses your senses; you are smelling lemongrass from the stick and tasting it where it permeated the meat during cooking.

The thing about Balinese cooking is that they use so many spices without things really being *spicy*, unlike Thai food, which for me is always at least a three-alarm kind of situation. It took some getting used to, because I was always asking for really hot chiles on the side until I finally learned to really appreciate their tricks, like using nutmeg in savory preparations and fresh turmeric root instead of dried powder. And unlike Thai satays, which are made with chicken breast strips, this satay uses ground dark-meat chicken.

I loved how the blend of spices and cooked shallots and garlic was completely fused with the chicken, molded around the lemongrass stalks, and then grilled until incredibly juicy. It also came with a sweetish, light, peanutty sauce that enhanced all the flavors instead of being cloying or gloppy, or covering them up. When I am there, I eat this twice a day, for both lunch and dinner. And when I'm not there, I make this version at home, which I've simplified a bit with some easier-to-find ingredients.

Chicken Satay, ok?

*Peel the papery layers off the lemongrass until you see the smooth, creamy-colored stalk. Cut off the hard root at the very end, and then finely mince that light-colored stalk.

Sauce

⅓ cup chunky peanut butter

¾ cup coconut milk

¼ cup fresh lime juice

1 tablespoon sugar

¼ teaspoon fish sauce

Skewers

2 tablespoons vegetable oil, plus more for greasing

3 medium shallots, finely minced

2 tablespoons finely minced fresh ginger (from about 1½-inch piece)

1 tablespoon finely minced garlic

1 large jalapeño pepper, finely minced (seeding optional)

1 teaspoon very finely minced lemongrass*

1½ teaspoons grated fresh turmeric, or ½ teaspoon ground turmeric

½ teaspoon ground white pepper

Pinch of grated nutmeg

Pinch of ground cloves

Pinch of ground allspice

1¼ pounds ground dark-meat chicken

¼ cup chopped fresh cilantro

2 tablespoons unsweetened shredded dried coconut

2 tablespoons light brown sugar

1 teaspoon kosher salt, plus more for seasoning

½ teaspoon fish sauce

6 whole lemongrass stalks, each cut into 3 (4-inch) lengths

1 MAKE THE SAUCE: Melt the peanut butter in a microwave-safe bowl for 15 seconds. Whisk in the coconut milk, lime juice, sugar, and fish sauce until smooth.

2 MAKE THE SKEWERS: Heat the oil in a medium skillet over medium-low heat. Add the shallots, ginger, garlic, jalapeño, and minced lemongrass and cook, stirring, until softened and fragrant, 1 to 2 minutes. Add the turmeric, pepper, nutmeg, cloves, and allspice and cook, stirring, 1 minute. Transfer to a mortar and pestle, cool for 5 minutes, then pound into a fine paste, 4 to 5 minutes (you can also puree it in a small food processor or bullet blender for 5 to 10 seconds).

3 Transfer the paste to a large bowl and add the ground chicken, cilantro, coconut, brown sugar, 1 teaspoon salt, and the fish sauce; mix until just combined. Cover and chill 30 minutes.

4 Divide the meat into 18 equal portions and mold each portion around a lemongrass stalk into a 3 × 2-inch patty about ½ inch thick. Heat a clean grill, grill pan, or large cast-iron skillet over medium heat. Lightly grease the grill grates or pan and grill the skewers until juicy and lightly charred, in batches if necessary, 2 to 3 minutes per side. Season to taste with salt and serve with the sauce.

herby eggplant dip

MAKES ABOUT 2 CUPS
ACTIVE TIME: 15 MINUTES
TOTAL TIME: 1 HOUR 50 MINUTES

If your experience with eggplant has been confined mostly to parmesan and antipasti (nothing to see here, folks), this dip might change your mind. I once had a sweet-smoky eggplant dip like this one at a dinner party. The whole meal was made by a "salad chef." I chummed it up with him, but when I texted him afterwards for some pointers, he ghosted me (which I kind of respect. Feed 'em and leave 'em!).

So, we figured it out on our own over here at Teigen Labs, and I have to say it's pretty damn close. When you cook eggplant with a little char, it takes on the teeniest bit of smokiness that is like a flavor all its own that you will find addictive! If you've got a grill, you can get it done there, or use your broiler or, if you're feeling a little pyro and messy, blacken those 'plants directly on your gas burners. Then make sure to let them cool almost completely and drain off all that juice (and there will be a lot!), which will make your dip meatier and less bitter. I added a bunch of herbs and some spice to make it really green and fresh—use whichever ones you have around the house!

2 medium to large eggplants (2½ pounds total)

¼ cup olive oil

1 tablespoon honey

2 teaspoons red wine vinegar, plus more as desired

¼ cup finely chopped fresh basil

¼ cup finely chopped scallion greens

¼ cup finely chopped fresh cilantro

1 small jalapeño pepper

1 teaspoon kosher salt, plus more for seasoning

1 Arrange a rack 5 inches from the broiler and preheat the broiler. Arrange the eggplants on a rimmed baking sheet and broil, turning once, until the skin is black and dry and the eggplant is slumped, 11 to 12 minutes per side. You can also do this on a grill set to high, or if you have gas burners, turn on the stove and put the eggplants right on the flames and turn them occasionally. The timing will change depending on which method you use, so just go with how it looks—totally blackened skin all over and soft all the way through.

2 Remove the eggplants to a colander set over a bowl and cool, letting any excess liquid drain out, at least 30 minutes. Peel the eggplants, then remove and discard as many seeds as you can (you should have about 2 cups eggplant pulp). Chop the eggplant, then add it to a bowl. In another bowl, whisk together the olive oil, honey, 2 teaspoons vinegar, basil, scallion greens, cilantro, jalapeño, and 1 teaspoon salt, then add to the eggplant and gently stir. Chill for 1 hour to let the flavors meld, then season to taste with more vinegar and salt.

hummus

with crispy garlic chips & spicy oil

SERVES 4 TO 6
ACTIVE TIME: 10 MINUTES
TOTAL TIME: 20 MINUTES

Hummus, hoo-moose, choo-muss. No matter how you pronounce it, you're talking chickpeas, blitzed until smooth and jacked up with little flavor pops to make it special. There is a whole shelf of the refrigerator case in every supermarket now dedicated to this Middle Eastern treat, and you can find some crazy flavors (chocolate? pumpkin spice? Hard pass). But this somewhat classic flavor profile pleased a crowd of tasters in our house and, more important, it pleased me, diehard hummus holdout who is slowwwwly learning to love chickpeas. The pasty, beige, and beany versions I got at the store never really did it for me, but I gotta say that now that we make it ourselves and eat it fresh, I am converted. I want anything I dip into to be packed with flavor, and this version is, thanks to lemon, garlic (and garlic oil!), cumin, and the LOML, salt. Little crispy garlic chips and a spicy oil topper seal this deal.

½ cup olive oil

5 garlic cloves

½ teaspoon cayenne pepper

1 (15-ounce) can chickpeas, drained, with ¼ cup liquid reserved

½ cup pure tahini*

¼ cup fresh lemon juice (from 1 large lemon)

1½ teaspoons kosher salt, plus more for seasoning

½ teaspoon ground cumin

Freshly ground black pepper

Chopped scallion greens, for garnish

Pita chips, for serving

1 Gently warm the olive oil in the smallest saucepan you have over medium-low heat. Thinly slice 3 of the garlic cloves. Test the oil by adding a garlic slice; if it sizzles right away and begins to brown, the oil is ready. Add the sliced garlic and cook until lightly browned and crisp, 2 to 3 minutes. Scoop out the garlic chips with a slotted spoon and drain on a paper towel; reserve the oil.

2 Place about 3 tablespoons of the still-warm oil in a small bowl and add the cayenne; let the rest of the garlic oil cool, and reserve.

3 Combine the chickpeas with their reserved liquid, the remaining 2 garlic cloves, the tahini, lemon juice, 2 tablespoons of the reserved garlic oil, the 1½ teaspoons salt, and the cumin in a food processor and process on high until fluffy and creamy, 3 minutes. Season to taste with more salt and pepper. Drizzle with the cayenne oil, then garnish with the scallion greens and garlic chips. Serve with pita chips on the side.

*Pure tahini is simply sesame seeds, usually roasted, ground into a paste. It comes in a jar or a white plastic container. Don't confuse it with prepared tahini, a seasoned dip/spread that comes in a tub similar to hummus.

spinach artie dip
in a
tortilla bowl

SERVES 4 TO 6
ACTIVE TIME: 10 MINUTES
TOTAL TIME: 45 MINUTES

"Chrissy! Didn't you already have an incredible spinach artichoke recipe in your other book!?" Why, yes, I sure did, and it's still one of the best bites I've ever made. It was all the greatness of spinach artie dip, blended with the spicy bites of juicy buffalo chicken. I still make it at least eight or ten times a year, but I remembered the Instagram complaints about it on an afternoon at Chili's the other day. (After reading that sentence, my editor asked, "Wait, so that dip was a Chili's reference?" And no, I meant I was literally just at Chili's the other day.) Anyway, anyone who made that recipe LOVED it, but those who didn't, didn't because it just seemed like a bit of a bitch to make for a dip. And I agree! It has lots of steps for a dish that gets entirely eaten in under 10 minutes.

So, enter THIS. This is another must-have household favorite, but rest easy—because this is sooooo much simpler. When we were developing it, Adeena popped this into the oven and left to take a call. She returned to the saddest little crumbs, never seeing how beautiful it looked plated, how stretchy every piece of toasty crust got. So, we just *haaaaaad* to make it again.

1 oversized (about 10-inch) flour tortilla*

2 tablespoons vegetable oil

¼ teaspoon kosher salt, plus more for seasoning

1 (10-ounce) package frozen chopped spinach, defrosted

1 (12-ounce) jar marinated artichoke hearts, drained, patted dry, and finely chopped

1 cup plus 3 tablespoons (5 ounces) shredded mozzarella cheese

1 cup (2 ounces) finely grated Parmigiano-Reggiano cheese

⅓ cup mayonnaise

3 tablespoons cream cheese, at room temperature

3 garlic cloves, minced

1 tablespoon minced jalapeño pepper, seeds included

1 teaspoon fish sauce

1 Preheat the oven to 325°F. Brush both sides of the tortilla with the oil, then season with ¼ teaspoon salt. Fit the tortilla inside a 6-inch oven-safe bowl or ramekin, trying to shape it inside the bowl with the sides standing up (to mimic a bowl or container). Bake until the edges are medium golden and the tortilla is dried out, 13 to 15 minutes. Remove from the oven, let cool for 3 minutes, then lift it out onto a foil-lined baking sheet (if the tortilla "bowl" doesn't hold, refit it into the bowl and bake for 2 more minutes).

2 Raise the oven temperature to 350°F. Wrap the spinach in paper towels and squeeze out all the excess moisture. Place the spinach in a medium bowl and combine with the artichoke hearts, 1 cup of the mozzarella, the parm, mayo, cream cheese, garlic, jalapeño, and fish sauce. Season to taste with salt. Spoon it into the tortilla bowl, sprinkle with the remaining 3 tablespoons mozzarella, and bake until the dip is stretchy and the tortilla bowl is golden brown, 25 to 30 minutes.

*If you want to make another tortilla into chips, brush both sides of a second tortilla with vegetable oil, season with salt, and use a pizza cutter to cut into chip-sized pieces. Arrange on a baking sheet and bake for the first 15 minutes along with the artie bowl.

roasted sesame party dip

SERVES 6
ACTIVE TIME: 5 MINUTES
TOTAL TIME: 20 MINUTES

This creamy, crunchy sesame party is like a deeply spiritual umami experience that f*cks with your brain on first contact. Your taste buds' initial impression will confuse you with a lil' onion dip vibe, but then you'll realize there is a very nutty sort of Asian-ish thing going on here, thanks to the soy sauce and fish sauce. (My mom Pepper always wonders where all her secret bottles of stinky delicious condiments disappear to, and this is exhibit A.)

The other secret ingredients are powdered onion and garlic, which give so many dips their perfect dippiness.

4 tablespoons sesame seeds

1 cup sour cream

½ cup mayonnaise

1½ teaspoons toasted sesame oil

1 teaspoon soy sauce

½ teaspoon fish sauce

2 teaspoons Dijon mustard

1 teaspoon onion powder

1 teaspoon garlic powder

¼ teaspoon cayenne pepper

3 tablespoons finely minced fresh chives

1 Preheat the oven to 350°F. Place the sesame seeds on a small, rimmed baking sheet and roast until a deep golden brown, 9 to 10 minutes. Transfer to a plate to cool.

2 Combine the sour cream, mayo, sesame oil, soy sauce, fish sauce, mustard, onion powder, garlic powder, and cayenne. Add 2 tablespoons of the sesame seeds and 2 tablespoons of the chives. You can serve immediately, but the flavors meld even more after an hour or two in the fridge. Garnish with the remaining 2 tablespoons roasted sesame seeds and remaining tablespoon chives just before serving.

yu tsai's lacy pan-fried dumplings

MAKES ABOUT 40 DUMPLINGS
ACTIVE TIME: 1 HOUR 5 MINUTES
TOTAL TIME: 1 HOUR 20 MINUTES
(INCLUDING MINIMUM CHILLING TIME)

One year, when I asked one of my favorite photographers, Yu Tsai, to shoot our family for the holidays, he asked to be let in early to set up.

We showed up expecting to find tripods, cameras, and lights, and we did, but we also found an incredible spread of produce from his family's orchards, candy boards that were the stuff of Instagram dreams, and these—the juiciest, most delicious dumplings we'd ever tasted, filled with flavorful pork and chives and with a lacy "skirt" like a thin crust that just barely holds the dumplings together. Yu simply can't help being over-the-top generous, and I gotta tell you it was like a rain shower of love in edible form. Another sign that Yu is someone special: he can coax a smile out of Miles when the rest of us are lucky to get a stink eye.

Anyway, I KNEW I had to taste those dumplings again, and we never thought we would be able to re-create them ourselves at home. But we were wrong! Because Yu then taught us how to make them, and they came out just as good as when he served them to us. So, trust me when I tell you that you can do this!

RECIPE CONTINUES

Dumplings

½ pound fatty ground pork*

4 ounces peeled and deveined shrimp, finely chopped

¼ cup finely minced fresh chives

1 cup very thinly sliced scallions (green and white parts)

1 tablespoon toasted sesame oil

1 tablespoon Shaoxing wine or dry sherry

1 tablespoon soy sauce

½ egg white (about 1 tablespoon)

½ tablespoon minced garlic

1½ teaspoons minced fresh ginger (from 1½-inch piece)

2 teaspoons cornstarch

1 teaspoon kosher salt

1 teaspoon sugar

½ teaspoon baking soda

¼ teaspoon ground white pepper

40 (4-inch) round dumpling wrappers**

Lacy Skirt

2½ cups water

10 teaspoons flour

2½ teaspoons rice vinegar

5 tablespoons vegetable oil

Hot sauce, sesame oil, soy sauce, or other dipping sauces of your choice, for serving

*If you can only find lean ground pork, use ¾ pound instead, and ask your butcher to grind ¼ pound pork fat, then mix the two and use half for the recipe.

1 **MAKE THE DUMPLINGS:** In a large bowl, gently combine all the dumpling ingredients except the wrappers. Mix until all is just incorporated. Press plastic wrap over the surface of the mixture and chill in the freezer for 15 minutes or in the fridge for 30 minutes or up to 4 hours.

2 When ready, fill a small bowl with a few tablespoons of water. Place a dumpling wrapper in the palm of your hand. Place about 2 teaspoons filling in the center of the wrapper, then use your fingers or a pastry brush to wet the edge of the wrapper with water. (Not too much! Just enough to moisten.) Pinch all the way across the dumpling wrapper to seal it together at the top. Then, using the center as your anchor, make accordion-like folds using your thumb and index finger to pinch the ½ inch of the dough on one side of the center back to the center of the dumpling, creating a fold. Fold and pinch 3 more times on that side, then repeat with 4 folds of the dumpling on the other side to form your adorable pouches. OR, to save time, you can just fold the dough over the filling, pinch it tight all the way across to seal it, and move on; they'll taste just as good!

**If you can't find 4-inch dumpling wrappers, you can cut rounds out of egg roll wrappers (which can be easier to find in some areas) using a 4-inch round cookie cutter. You'll need at least an 18-ounce package of egg roll wrappers.

3 **MAKE THE LACY SKIRT:** For each batch of 8 dumplings, whisk ½ cup water, 2 teaspoons flour, and ½ teaspoon vinegar in a bowl until cloudy and the flour is dissolved.

4 Heat an 8- or 9-inch nonstick skillet with a tight-fitting lid over medium-high heat for 2 minutes. Add 1 tablespoon of the oil and heat 1 additional minute. Add 8 dumplings to the skillet without overlapping and fry until the underside is browned, 2 minutes. Restir the skirt mixture, pour it into the skillet between the dumplings, cover, reduce the heat to medium, and cook until the skirt slurry forms a holey layer, about 6 minutes. Uncover to let the remaining liquid evaporate, until the lacy skirt is browned and crisp, another 2 to 3 minutes.

5 Use oven mitts to cover the skillet with a plate and flip the dumplings onto the plate. Repeat with the remaining 4 batches of 8 dumplings, using 1 tablespoon oil and a fresh lacy skirt mixture per batch. Serve the dumplings right away, with dipping sauces. Uncooked dumplings can be frozen and cooked right from the freezer.

sweet & spicy

thai beef jerky

SERVES 6 TO 8
ACTIVE TIME: 15 MINUTES
TOTAL TIME: 2 HOURS (INCLUDING MARINATING TIME)

I don't wanna brag, but I'm a *bit* of a jerky expert. The origins of my knowledge come from hours and hours spent on road trips, in and out of Flying J truck stops, snapping away on Slim Jims or gnawing on the same piece of Oh Boy! Oberto till it was like a wet piece of meat fabric in my mouth. I know how delicious that sounds, but if you know, you *know*.

Eventually, thanks to a South African boyfriend, I graduated from jerky to biltong, which is thinly sliced, cured pieces of WHATEVER—ostrich, beef, fish, anything. I would always ask the butcher for the juiciest little nuggets, pieces that were bright white with fat ready to melt in your mouth.

But if I'm being honest, my heart has always belonged to warm, sweet Thai jerky made from soy- and brown sugar–marinated skirt steak. I would form a ball of hot sticky rice between my fingers and stick a chunk to every single dried, flavorful morsel of beauty until it became more of a meal than a snack.

Here, we bring the street version right to your home—sweet, spicy, simple to make; you just bake the marinated meat until it's dry, and then give it a quick fry. The thinner strips are crisp, while the thicker steak pieces have more chew and a meatier texture. Both are delicious, with crispy, caramelized edges that are just on the edge of burnt. Feel free to taste-test alongside any jerky you previously thought was delicious. We win, or your money back!!

1 In a large bowl, whisk together the brown sugar, soy sauce, oyster sauce, sesame oil, red pepper flakes, and MSG.

2 Cut the steak against the grain into 1-inch-wide strips. If you need to, cut longer whole pieces of steak into 4-inch squares or rectangles, and then cut them so you can keep cutting against the grain. Add the steak pieces to the marinade, toss to evenly coat, and let sit at room temperature for 30 minutes.

3 Preheat the oven to 200°F. Arrange a rack on a rimmed baking sheet and spray with nonstick cooking spray. Arrange the beef in a single layer on the rack, separated if possible (it will shrink so don't worry too much). Discard any excess marinade. Bake until the meat appears drier and has shrunk a bit, 1 hour.

4 Line a baking sheet or large plate with paper towels. Heat 2 inches of oil in a large (at least 4-quart) pot until it reaches 350°F on a deep-fry thermometer, or until a small piece of meat begins to sizzle and cook right away.

5 Working in batches, fry the meat, stirring it as it cooks, until it darkens and crisps, 45 seconds to 1 minute. Drain on paper towels and let cool at least 10 minutes before eating. The longer it cools, the crispier and chewier the jerky becomes. (Store in a sealed container in the fridge for up to 1 week.)

⅓ cup (lightly packed) dark brown sugar

2 tablespoons soy sauce

1 tablespoon oyster sauce

1 tablespoon toasted sesame oil

¾ teaspoon red pepper flakes

¾ teaspoon MSG (see note, page 105)

2 pounds boneless beef skirt steak

Vegetable oil, for frying

spicy salmon
krispy rice

SERVES 4 TO 6 AS AN APPETIZER
ACTIVE TIME: 25 MINUTES
TOTAL TIME: 1 HOUR 10 MINUTES (INCLUDING SOAKING TIME)

Krispy Rice, the sushi-baby brainchild of the people behind Katsuya (one of our favorite Japanese spots), has been a delivery godsend in L.A. I had been eating the stuff for a while when I did what any admirer worth her wasabi would do—I slid into their DMs. Eventually they came to teach our Covid-year school pod and our verrry confused preschoolers how to make a perfect roll of sushi. I was on bedrest when it happened, but I kept hearing total glorious chaos erupting downstairs. The photos poured in and my jealousy/FOMO raged . . . until pure deliciousness, in the form of a little block of crispy (er, KRISPY) rice blanketed in the creamiest, spiciest salmon of all time, was hand-delivered straight to my mouth.

We managed to drag Chef Lester back to the office to teach us how to make these babies, and now YOU can have the most divine bite of your life any time you want.

Thank you for sharing your secrets, Krispy Rice! We love you!

Rice

¼ cup unseasoned rice vinegar

2 tablespoons sugar

1½ teaspoons kosher salt

1 cup sushi rice

1¼ cups water

Salmon

⅔ cup Kewpie or regular mayonnaise

1 tablespoon Sriracha

1½ teaspoons hot chili oil

1 teaspoon sugar

1 teaspoon blond miso paste (such as Miso Master Mellow White)

1 teaspoon ponzu sauce (or lime juice)

8 ounces very fresh ("sushi-grade") skinless salmon, very finely minced

½ teaspoon toasted sesame oil

1 tablespoon masago* (capelin) or salmon roe

2 teaspoons very finely minced scallion greens, plus some sliced greens for garnish

Kosher salt

¼ cup vegetable oil, plus more for oiling your hands and the plate

*These tiny red fish eggs are the same ones that make your sushi look so pretty! If you can't find masago in a store, include an order of red tobiko sushi in your next delivery order, then scrape it off and use it here. You can also use ikura (salmon roe) and you can also skip it altogether!

1 MAKE THE RICE: Combine the vinegar, sugar, and salt in a small bowl and microwave until the sugar is dissolved, 30 to 45 seconds.

2 Place the rice in a colander and run under cold running water until the starch is rinsed away and the water runs clear, 2 to 3 minutes. Place the rice in a bowl, cover with cold water, and soak for 20 minutes.

3 Drain the rice well, place in a small saucepan, cover with the 1¼ cups water, and bring to a boil over medium-high heat, stirring often so the rice doesn't stick to the bottom of the pot. Cover, reduce the heat to a very low simmer, and cook until all the water is absorbed, 13 to 15 minutes. Transfer the rice to a medium bowl to cool for a few minutes, then gently stir in the vinegar mixture 1 tablespoon at a time until absorbed. Gently press plastic wrap onto the surface of the rice and let the rice hang out while you make the salmon.

4 MAKE THE SALMON: In a small bowl, combine the mayo, Sriracha, 1 teaspoon of the chili oil, the sugar, miso, and ponzu.

5 In a medium bowl, gently combine the salmon with 2 tablespoons of the mayo mixture (save the rest for sandwiches, as a sauce for tempura, or for this recipe when you make it again), sesame oil, masago, remaining ½ teaspoon chili oil, and the 2 teaspoons scallion greens. Season to taste with salt and refrigerate while you crisp the rice.

6 **MAKE THE KRISPY RICE**: Using lightly oiled hands, measure 2½ tablespoons rice and form it into a 2 × 1-inch rectangle ½ inch thick and arrange on a lightly oiled plate. Repeat with the remaining rice to yield about 15 rice blocks. Heat the ¼ cup oil in a 9-inch nonstick skillet over medium heat. Add half the rice blocks to the skillet and cook, sliding the blocks around occasionally to brown evenly, until the undersides are crisp and golden, 4 to 6 minutes. Don't flip them! Drain them on paper towels and repeat with the remaining rice blocks.

7 Spoon about 1 tablespoon of the spicy salmon mixture on the untoasted side of each rice block, molding it to fit the shape of the rice. Garnish with more sliced scallion greens.

shrimp & tuna

coconut ceviche on wonton crisps

MAKES 8 STACKS
ACTIVE TIME: 40 MINUTES
TOTAL TIME: 1 HOUR 40 MINUTES (INCLUDING CHILLING TIME)

Food on an edible plate is a genius concept that knows no cultural boundaries. Tostadas, topped noodle cakes . . . food atop crispy food is just brilliant—like this ceviche on fried wonton skins. Wonton wrappers come in packages of, like, 8 zillion in a little shrink-wrapped cube, and frying them and watching them puff up like magic is one of the most soothing activities ever! (They fry really fast, so be sure to remove them from the oil while they're still a medium-golden brown, because they'll continue to darken on those oil-draining paper towels.)

Aside from bottoming this no-cook shrimp-and-tuna number, with its hint of coconut and lime, a sweet pop of mango, and the inevitable Teigen hint of spice, these won-ton-ton-ton-tons are the best tortilla-chip replacement on earth. Just ask those of us who stood in my office late one night, using them to desperately hoover up guacamole. The moral of the story here is: make extra fried wonton skins and store them in an airtight container.

½ pound peeled and deveined uncooked shrimp, diced small

½ pound sushi-grade tuna, diced small

7 tablespoons fresh lime juice (from 3 small limes), plus more as desired

1 cup diced fresh mango (from 1 medium)*

½ cup unsweetened coconut milk

Finely grated zest of 1 lime

2 teaspoons light brown sugar, plus more as desired

1 teaspoon fish sauce, plus more for seasoning

½ teaspoon kosher salt, plus more for seasoning

½ cup chopped fresh cilantro, plus leaves for garnish

1 teaspoon finely minced red or green jalapeño pepper (seeded, if desired)

Vegetable oil, for frying

17 (3-inch-square) wonton wrappers

*Google up a video to see how to cut up a mango; it's honestly easiest that way.

1 In a medium glass, ceramic, or stainless-steel bowl, combine the shrimp, tuna, and 4 tablespoons lime juice and toss to coat. Refrigerate, tossing 2 or 3 times, until the shrimp is opaque and the tuna lightens in color, about 40 minutes.

2 Strain the liquid from the seafood and discard. Add the mango cubes to the shrimp and tuna and toss. In another medium bowl, whisk together the coconut milk, remaining 3 tablespoons lime juice, the lime zest, brown sugar, fish sauce, and ½ teaspoon salt. Add to the shrimp and tuna mixture, toss to coat, and fold in the cilantro and jalapeño. Season with more lime juice as desired.

3 Arrange some paper towels on a baking sheet. Heat 2 inches of the vegetable oil in a medium saucepan over medium heat. Tear a wonton wrapper into strips. When the oil is hot and looks wavy (about 400°F), drop in a strip; if it begins to puff and turn golden immediately, the oil is ready.

4 Working with 2 or 3 wrappers at a time, add them to the oil and fry until they puff and turn light golden, flipping once, 15 to 20 seconds total. Remove with a Chinese spider or other slotted spoon and drain on the paper towels. Season with salt.

5 Arrange the wonton chips on a serving tray and serve with the ceviche. Garnish with cilantro.

crispy vegetable tempura with wasabi soy mayo

SERVES 4 TO 6
ACTIVE TIME: 45 MINUTES
TOTAL TIME: 45 MINUTES

I order the tempura for home delivery every damn time I see it. I need to stop! Because the risk of sog-out for any fried food trying to make it from the restaurant to my couch is high. It's a real problem.

But lucky for me I have this incredible tempura recipe we now make at home. It makes everything taste like a puff of flavory goodness—the actual tempura batter itself has flavor! When I do get it for delivery, my standing order is shrimp and vegetables, but I actually prefer the vegetables. I find myself going for the onion, the sweet potato, the asparagus, the shiitakes . . . and now, THE CORN. Yes, you heard me. I am personally not into the ponzu sauce that usually comes with the tempura (though you might be!), so here I whipped up a nice little flavored mayo to go with it.

Sauce

¼ cup Kewpie or regular mayonnaise

1 teaspoon wasabi paste,
or ½ teaspoon wasabi powder

1 teaspoon low-sodium soy sauce

Tempura

Vegetable oil, for frying

1 egg

1 tablespoon mayonnaise, preferably
Kewpie

1 tablespoon vodka (optional)

1 cup very cold seltzer or club soda

½ cup all-purpose flour, plus more
for dredging

½ cup rice flour

1½ teaspoons kosher salt, plus more
for seasoning

4 (4-inch) ears corn-on-the-cob, or
2 full-size ears, cooked, cooled, and
patted dry

1 (4-ounce) baby eggplant, cut on
the diagonal into ⅛-inch slices

1 (4-ounce) orange sweet potato,
peeled and cut on the diagonal into
⅛-inch slices

1 (4-ounce) package fresh whole
shiitake mushrooms, stemmed

½ medium onion, cut into 2-inch
wedges and separated into petals

1 MAKE THE SAUCE: Combine the mayo, wasabi, and soy sauce in a small bowl. Set aside.

2 MAKE THE BATTER AND FRY: Fill a large skillet that has high sloping sides, or at least a 4-quart pot, halfway with vegetable oil and heat the oil over medium heat to 375°F. (Use a frying thermometer.) Heat the oven to 175°F and have a sheet pan or baking sheet ready.

3 In a large bowl, whisk the egg and mayo together, then gently stir in the vodka, if using, followed by the seltzer (everything will froth a bit). Add the ½ cup flour, the rice flour, and 1½ teaspoons salt and whisk gently until it resembles lumpy pancake batter. In a shallow medium bowl, spread out a few tablespoons of the flour for dredging.

4 Stand one of the ears of corn on its end. Using a sharp chef's knife, cut the kernels off from top to bottom, cutting into the cob itself a bit to help keep the kernels together in little sheets. Handle these with extra care, as you want to retain the corn in sheets!

5 Dredge the eggplant, sweet potatoes, mushrooms, onion, and corn a few at a time in the flour, then shake off the excess and drop them into the batter and stir to coat on all sides. Pull the vegetables out with a fork or chopsticks, letting the excess batter drip off.

6 Gently lower the coated veggies into the oil a few pieces at a time and fry, turning often, until puffed, crispy, and very pale golden, 2 to 3 minutes per batch, adjusting the oil temperature to maintain a temp between 350°F and 375°F.

7 Drain the vegetables on a paper towel–lined plate, then keep warm on the sheet pan in the warm oven while you fry more batches. Season with salt and serve with the sauce.

noodles + carbs

lemony angel hair

with ricotta & pine nuts

SERVES 2 TO 3
ACTIVE TIME: 20 MINUTES
TOTAL TIME: 25 MINUTES

I've been disappointed so many times by angel hair pasta, but over time, I have come to realize it wasn't the pasta's fault. It's just that it's often covered in sauces much too heavy, much too wrong for the delicate threads of this, the thinnest pasta. But when treated with hands of velvet, cashmere, lambskin, whatever, angel hair can be beautiful, Rapunzel-esque strands of perfection.

My angel hair is tart with fresh lemon juice, but with the warm hug of butter. The stirring-in of cream and ricotta makes for swirls and swirls of fatty love, perfectly complementing that lemon juice you worked sooooo hard to squeeze. Yes! That was hard work. It's still 2020 as I write this. Everything is harder, okay?

2 large lemons

½ cup ricotta

3 tablespoons olive oil, plus more for drizzling

1½ teaspoons kosher salt, plus more for seasoning

2 tablespoons unsalted butter

4 garlic cloves, very thinly sliced

⅔ cup heavy cream

½ pound dry angel hair pasta

2 tablespoons toasted pine nuts

2 tablespoons chopped fresh parsley

Freshly ground black pepper

1 Bring a large pot of generously salted water to a boil. Use a peeler to peel thick strips of the zest from half of one of the lemons, then add the peels to the water as it comes to a boil.

2 Use a fine grater, like a microplane, to zest the remaining half of that lemon and stir it into the ricotta along with 1 tablespoon of the olive oil and a little salt to taste. Zest the other lemon and reserve. Juice both lemons (you should have about 6 tablespoons of juice).

3 In a large skillet, heat 1 tablespoon each of the olive oil and the butter over medium-low heat. Add the garlic and cook, stirring, until softened but not browned, 3 minutes.

4 Add the cream, reserved lemon zest, remaining tablespoon butter, and 1½ teaspoons salt to the skillet. Raise the heat to medium-high and cook until the cream is bubbling, then reduce the heat to medium and cook until a little more thickened, 1 to 2 more minutes. Remove from the heat and cover with foil to keep warm.

5 Drop the pasta into the boiling water and cook until just undercooked, about 2½ minutes. (Angel hair is so thin, it will definitely finish cooking, don't worry!) Drain the pasta, add it to the warm cream, then add 5 tablespoons of the lemon juice and toss through the pasta. Season to taste with more lemon juice and salt.

6 Divide the pasta among bowls, dollop with the lemon-flavored ricotta, drizzle with the remaining tablespoon olive oil, and top with pine nuts and parsley. Sprinkle with pepper just before serving.

perfectly pink pasta

SERVES 4 TO 6 (OR, LIKE, 10 LITTLE KIDS)
ACTIVE TIME: 10 MINUTES
TOTAL TIME: 30 MINUTES

Listen, before I had kids, I was dead set that my attitude toward feeding them would absolutely be: "If you don't eat what I put in front of you, you WILL be going to bed hungry!" Fast-forward to that attitude definitely not f*cking working, and I've done everything possible to get my kids to eat what I make, short of shaving my head and gluing macaroni onto it.

Luna is extremely against things touching things or things in things, as any reasonably psychotic toddler is, so instead of rattling her world with some sort of chicken alfredo or basil marinara, we decided to go for a perfectly uniform, smooth sauce that is still delightfully tasty while being different enough from the jarred pasta sauce we so desperately want to grab for sheer ease.

Caramelizing the tomato paste is the move that gives it extra sweetness, a secret dash of fish sauce bumps up the umami, the cream rounds out the acidity of the tomatoes, and the sauce magically finds this way of sticking to every part of the pasta you choose, whether it be fusilli, bucatini (my favorite), penne, or spaghetti. It is THE perfect sauce: easy to double or triple for storing in the freezer, ready to go whenever desired. If you must adult it, go ahead and add some dried Italian seasoning, sprinkle on some red pepper flakes, slip in some browned sausage—but then feed to *your* Luna at your own risk.

2 tablespoons olive oil

3 or 4 garlic cloves, minced

2 tablespoons tomato paste

1 (26-ounce) container strained tomatoes, such as Pomi

2 teaspoons kosher salt, plus more for seasoning

1 teaspoon fish sauce (or 1 more teaspoon kosher salt)

1 teaspoon Italian seasoning

½ teaspoon sugar

½ teaspoon red wine vinegar

⅔ cup heavy cream

1 (1-pound) box fusilli pasta

½ cup finely grated Parmigiano-Reggiano cheese

Fresh basil, for garnish

1 Bring a large pot of generously salted water to boil.

2 Meanwhile, in a medium-large saucepan, heat the olive oil over low to medium-low heat. Add the garlic and cook, stirring, until fragrant, 3 minutes. Add the tomato paste and cook, stirring, until caramelized and a shade darker, 2 minutes.

3 Add the strained tomatoes, the 2 teaspoons kosher salt, the fish sauce, Italian seasoning, sugar, and red wine vinegar. Bring to a boil, reduce the heat to low, and simmer until the sauce thickens slightly, 10 minutes. Stir in the cream, simmer another 2 minutes, then remove from the heat and cover to keep warm.

4 Cook the pasta in the boiling water according to package instructions until al dente. Drain, reserving a little pasta water, then add the pasta to the sauce, toss to coat, and loosen with a bit of the pasta water if you like, then season to taste with salt.

5 Divide the pasta among bowls, and garnish with the cheese and basil.

Mooooore Cheese, Please

Try adding about 4 ounces of fresh mozzarella, cut into small cubes, into the pasta along with the sauce, and toss just to combine, about 10 seconds.

baked pasta
with ham
& peas

SERVES 6 AS AN APPETIZER OR 3 TO 4 AS A MAIN COURSE
ACTIVE TIME: 15 MINUTES
TOTAL TIME: 25 MINUTES

Okay. I consider all my recipes to be my babies, but some have a fully built home in my heart. This is one of those recipes that floods my brain with happy memories. For a few years, early in my relationship with John, we lived in a tiny (truly tiny) hotel-like room above restaurant Cipriani on Wall Street, in New York. There weren't a lot of apartments in this neighborhood, so it was always empty at night. I was used to the character of the Lower East Side, and now I was surrounded by shoeshine storefronts and bars packed with finance dudes.

I remember going down to Cipriani after their busy lunchtimes and sitting alone, soaking in the big empty room, always ordering their baked tagliolini. Hooooooooly shit, it's truly one of the best dishes I have ever eaten. Creamy-creamy sauce, strands of ham, and perfectly cooked pasta that somehow doesn't get *overcooked* under the broiler. I've simplified the dish a bit here, but I can confidently say IT IS PERFECTION. It's insanely saucy and decadent as is, but feel free to toss in extra peas or sauté your ham in butter, just like they do at Cipriani. Get ready to marvel at the broiled, hot, bubbling cheesy cream. Ennnnjoy!!

3 tablespoons unsalted butter

3 garlic cloves, minced

2 tablespoons flour

1 cup light cream, half-and-half, or heavy cream (or a combination)

1 cup whole milk

½ teaspoon kosher salt, plus more for seasoning

¼ teaspoon grated nutmeg

1½ cups (3 ounces) freshly grated Parmigiano-Reggiano cheese, plus more for sprinkling

½ pound fresh tagliatelle or tagliolini pasta*

1 cup frozen peas, defrosted

2 ounces very thinly sliced deli ham of your choice

1 Bring a large pot of well-salted water to a boil.

2 Heat 2 tablespoons of the butter in a medium saucepan over low heat. Add the garlic and flour and cook, stirring, until fragrant but not browned, 2 to 3 minutes. Add the cream, milk, ½ teaspoon salt, and the nutmeg, bring to a boil, reduce the heat to a high simmer and cook until the mixture thickens, 2 to 3 minutes. Stir in the 1½ cups cheese until smooth. Taste, and add more salt, if necessary. Remove from the heat and cover to keep warm.

3 Set a rack 5 to 6 inches under the broiler and preheat the broiler. Cook the pasta in the boiling water until al dente, 2 to 3 minutes. Drain well, then toss in a bowl with the remaining tablespoon butter. Place the pasta in a heavy 9-inch skillet, add the peas and ham, and toss them right in the skillet. Pour the sauce on top and use tongs to move the pasta around to coat it with the sauce. Scatter a little more cheese on top, then place under the broiler and broil until bubbling and the top is deep golden in parts, 6 to 8 minutes.

*If you don't have fresh pasta, use ½ pound dried egg fettuccine and cook according to package directions.

cheesy spinach stuffed shells

with roasted red pepper tomato sauce

SERVES 3 TO 4
ACTIVE TIME: 20 MINUTES
TOTAL TIME: 1 HOUR

You guys hear "stuffed shells," and I can't even type what happens to your jeans. People go crazy! I posted a version of these on my Instagram, and for a week after, I swear to you, I kept hearing that it was impossible to find jumbo shells in the store anymore. The dish was a hit because it was so easy—canned tomato sauce, jarred pesto, pre-shredded cheese. And sure! That was good. Very good. But why not have great? Or VERY GREAT?

Here it is; the big upgrade is a roasted red pepper–tomato sauce. Double, triple, quadruple this sauce to freeze for meals to come (and, in particular, for the Mile-High-Worthy Veggie-Stuffed Poblanos, page 217). If you want more sauce in this dish, go ahead and use some of the extra, but I go a little light here because I like the edges of the pasta to crisp and the cheese to ooze without the disturbance of sauce overload. I wanted these shells to shine and show themselves in all their glory!

18 jumbo pasta shells

1 teaspoon olive oil

1 (24-ounce) jar good-quality marinara sauce

1 (15-ounce) jar fire-roasted peppers, drained, rinsed, and drained again (about 2 cups; see note on page 218)

1½ teaspoons kosher salt, plus more as needed

1 pound whole-milk ricotta

2 cups (4 ounces) shredded mozzarella cheese

1½ cups (3 ounces) finely grated Parmigiano-Reggiano cheese

1 (10-ounce) package frozen chopped spinach, defrosted and squeezed of excess liquid

1 teaspoon garlic powder

1 teaspoon dried oregano

½ teaspoon dried thyme

¼ teaspoon red pepper flakes

1 Preheat the oven to 375°F. Bring a large pot of generously salted water to a boil. Cook the shells according to package directions, drain, and toss with the olive oil to prevent sticking.

2 In a blender or food processor, combine the marinara, peppers, and ½ teaspoon of the salt and process until smooth, 15 to 20 seconds. You should have about 4½ cups of sauce; divide the sauce in half and save the other half for another time.

3 Coat the bottom of a 9 × 13-inch baking dish with 1½ cups of the sauce. In a large bowl, combine the ricotta, 1 cup each of the mozz and parm, the spinach, garlic powder, oregano, thyme, red pepper flakes, and remaining 1 teaspoon salt, and mix until incorporated. Stuff each shell with 2½ to 3 tablespoons of the cheese mixture and arrange them in rows on top of the sauce. Drizzle with the remaining ¾ cup sauce and top with the remaining 1 cup mozz and ½ cup parm.

4 Cover and bake 30 minutes, then uncover and bake until the cheese is bubbling and the edges of the pasta are lightly browned, another 10 to 12 minutes.

sour-dough jack hamburger helper

SERVES 8 TO 10
ACTIVE TIME: 35 MINUTES
TOTAL TIME: 1 HOUR 15 MINUTES

It's no secret, my love for fast food. My love for the mystery tacos at Jack in the Box, the beauty that is the Sourdough Jack sandwich. The comfort those things bring me is indescribable, but whatever the f*ck we have done here is nothing short of *incredible*.

We somehow (wait, I know how and I will show you how!) made something that is exactly, *exactly*, like biting into the best part of the Sourdough Jack—the center—but it's in every single bite of this casserole: the oozy creaminess and cheese, the tomato, the bacon, the juicy beef all mixed with macaroni, with sourdough bread crumbs for a little punch.

3 cups uncooked elbow macaroni

3 tablespoons plus 1 teaspoon unsalted butter, melted

12 ounces thick-cut bacon

1½ pounds lean ground beef

1 large yellow onion, chopped

2 tablespoons minced garlic

¼ cup flour

5 cups whole milk

2 teaspoons kosher salt, plus more for seasoning

½ teaspoon freshly ground black pepper

2 cups (8 ounces) shredded Swiss cheese

2½ cups diced tomatoes, with juice

3 (1-inch-thick) slices sourdough bread (or six ½-inch slices)

2 tablespoons minced chives

1 Bring a large pot of generously salted water to a boil over medium-high heat. Cook the pasta 1 minute less than for al dente, according to package directions. Drain well and place it in a large bowl. Add 1 teaspoon of the melted butter and toss to coat well.

2 Preheat the oven to 375°F. In a large (5-quart) Dutch oven over medium heat, cook the bacon, turning occasionally, until crisp, about 10 minutes. Drain on paper towels, leaving the fat in the pot. Add the ground beef and cook over medium heat, breaking it up with a wooden spoon, until no longer pink, 5 to 6 minutes.

3 Set a colander inside a medium bowl and drain the beef. Return 3 tablespoons of the cooking liquid and fat to the pot and discard the rest. Add the onion and cook over medium heat, stirring often, until lightly golden, 9 to 10 minutes. Add the garlic and cook, stirring, 1 minute. Return the beef to the skillet, then add the flour and cook, stirring, 1 to 2 minutes.

4 Add the milk, 1¾ teaspoons of the salt, and the pepper and bring to a boil over medium-high heat, stirring occasionally and scraping the bottom of the pot. Reduce the heat to medium-low and simmer, stirring, until the mixture thickens, 3 to 4 minutes. Crumble the bacon and stir it into the pot along with the cheese and tomatoes, then gently fold in the noodles. Season to taste with salt and remove from heat.

5 Tear the bread into large chunks and process in a food processor until bread crumbs form, 15 seconds (it's okay if a few of the chunks are bigger). In a medium bowl, toss the crumbs with the remaining 3 tablespoons melted butter and ¼ teaspoon salt, then top the noodles with the bread crumbs and bake, uncovered, until the noodle mixture bubbles around the edges and the bread crumbs are golden and toasty, 35 to 40 minutes. Let cool for 5 minutes, then garnish with the chives.

creamy corn & truffle pasta

SERVES 4
ACTIVE TIME: 10 MINUTES
TOTAL TIME: 25 MINUTES

From my vantage point, Malibu, which is on the West Side in L.A., might as well be Russia. But there is a place in that land far, far away that makes it worth facing traffic, and that place is the one and only Giorgio Baldi. It's dark. It's romantic. It's so Italian! The memories of GB have carried us through almost a year's worth of non–date-night existence without the excitement of getting dressed and hiding in a corner and canoodling while noodling. Because Giorgio Baldi is home to one of the most incredible bites I have ever had: sweet corn agnolotti with mascarpone, Parm, and a snowdrift of fresh white truffles when they are in season. They're like tiny pillows that you put in your mouth one by one to let all the flavors just travel all over your taste buds.

What we have done here is so reminiscent of that, but so much easier than making and stuffing from-scratch pasta. The sweet corn really comes through, the sauce is creamy, and—this is the most I will ever ask of you—if you can, splurge on a fresh truffle! A little goes a long way, but of course, if that's not in your plans, feel free to use a little truffle oil instead. When you take a bite of this dish it is so sweet, sort of like pasta for dessert. Which is really fitting, because at Giorgio Baldi, I don't order dessert—I just order another pasta.

2 cups drained canned white sweet corn kernels (or thawed frozen kernels)

2 tablespoons low-sodium chicken broth (or vegetable broth or water)

½ cup mascarpone cheese

1 teaspoon kosher salt, plus more for seasoning

12 ounces bucatini pasta

6 tablespoons unsalted butter

1½ ounces Parmigiano-Reggiano cheese, finely grated (¾ cup), plus more for garnish

½ teaspoon fresh lemon juice

¼ ounce fresh white truffle* (or a drizzle of truffle oil)

Freshly ground black pepper

1 Puree the corn and broth in a blender on high speed until totally smooth, 1 to 1½ minutes. Add the mascarpone and 1 teaspoon salt and blend until incorporated and smooth, 15 seconds.

2 Bring a large pot of generously salted water to a boil. Add the pasta and cook until al dente, according to package directions.

3 While the pasta is cooking, add the butter to a large skillet with tall sloping sides (you'll be tossing the sauce and pasta in there) and cook over medium heat until the butter turns frothy, then small brown bits form, 3 to 4 minutes. Transfer 2 tablespoons of the browned butter to a small bowl. Add the corn-mascarpone puree to the butter remaining in the skillet and warm over medium-low heat.

4 When the pasta is cooked, drain it, reserving ¼ cup of the cooking water. Add the pasta to the sauce and toss to coat, adding a little splash of cooking water to loosen the mixture. Add the parm and the lemon juice, then grate some truffle into the pasta and toss to coat, seasoning with more salt to taste.

5 Divide the pasta among 4 bowls, then drizzle a little of the reserved browned butter over each serving. Grate a touch more truffle on top of each bowl and top with a bit more parm and some black pepper.

*These are verrry expensive and might make you hate me for being bougie, but if you have ever had a white truffle, ohhhh, you will want them as much as I do during truffle season, when they're flown in from Italy. Otherwise, you can use a drop or two of truffle oil, which is easier to find and much more affordable.

pizza bianca
(white pizza) with cheese-roasted garlic

MAKES 2 PIZZAS, EACH SERVING 2 TO 3
ACTIVE TIME: 15 MINUTES
TOTAL TIME: 1 HOUR 15 MINUTES
(INCLUDING SINGLE RISING TIME)

At a time when we all need something relaxing and meditative, it can feel so calming and so satisfying to turn flour and water into something squishy . . . and then delicious. I know, I know, the idea of making your own dough for pizza can feel intimidating, the opposite of relaxing, but relax! This dough is magic: it's fast, it's simple, it's foolproof. We got you!

Of course, you could do a classic topping here with tomato sauce and fresh mozz, but we went bianca (white), because white pizzas are so darn comforting to look at—the blank canvas our brains need right now. We threw on mozz, ricotta, and parm, and slices of garlic, which self-roast as the pizza bakes.

P.S.: Yes, you can double the recipe, and yes, you can freeze one ball of fully risen dough, then defrost it later for a perfect pie.

Dough

1 cup warm water

1½ tablespoons sugar

1 tablespoon active dry yeast

2 tablespoons olive oil, plus more as needed

2 teaspoons kosher salt

2⅔ cups flour, plus more as needed

Topping
(double if baking 2 pizzas)

2½ tablespoons olive oil

Kosher salt

1 cup (4 ounces) grated mozzarella cheese

½ cup (1 ounce) finely shredded Parmigiano-Reggiano cheese

½ cup fresh ricotta

Red pepper flakes

2 garlic cloves, thinly sliced

Freshly ground black pepper

1 MAKE THE DOUGH: In a large bowl, stir the warm water and sugar together, then sprinkle the yeast over it and let rest for 5 minutes; if it gets fluffy and frothy, you're ready to move on. If not, it means you need to start again with new yeast, or with warm-but-not-hot water. (Too-hot water, like water that you don't want your finger in, will kill the yeast.) Add the olive oil, then add the salt and flour, and stir with a wooden spoon until a sticky but single piece of dough forms.

2 Lightly flour your clean workspace and scoop out the dough onto it. Knead the dough until smooth but not dry, adding flour by the tablespoonful if it's too sticky to work with (you shouldn't need much). I could try to describe to you how to do the motions to knead the dough if you don't know how, but honestly, it's easier to just Google up a video. This is a pretty simple dough, and any kneading method will basically work! Lightly oil a bowl, then transfer the dough to the bowl, cover with plastic wrap, and let rest in a warm place until the dough gets puffy, 30 to 45 minutes.

3 At this point, you're ready to bake, or you can put the dough in the fridge to use later, or you can freeze it (see "Make Ahead"). Let it come to near room temperature before using it.

4 About 30 minutes before cooking, place a large (at least

12-inch) dry cast-iron skillet in the oven and preheat it to 525°F. Uncover the dough, then divide it into two pieces. If you're using both, keep the second piece covered with plastic wrap while you work with the first (if not, you can now wrap the second piece in plastic wrap and freeze it).

5 Arrange a 12-inch square of aluminum foil on a clean work surface. Brush 1 tablespoon olive oil onto the foil, leaving a 1-inch unbrushed border. Place the dough in the center of the foil, flatten slightly, then use another tablespoon of oil to help you spread the dough into a 11-inch circle, leaving the outside slightly thicker (like a pizza crust!). Season with salt. Use oven mitts to take the skillet out of the oven (it is insanely hot!!) and arrange the foil-lined crust in the skillet. Return the skillet to the oven and bake until the crust is slightly browned and parbaked, 6 to 7 minutes.

6 Remove the crust from the oven and sprinkle the mozz and parm over the crust, then dollop with the ricotta. Sprinkle with the red pepper flakes and garlic slices, aiming the garlic at the cheese so that the cheese fat helps sizzle the garlic. Return to the oven and bake until the cheese bubbles and the crust puffs and is dark brown in spots, another 5 to 6 minutes. Remove from the oven, drizzle with the remaining ½ tablespoon oil, and season generously with salt and pepper.

make ahead

To save the dough for later, brush a piece of plastic wrap lightly with olive oil. Deflate the risen dough by punching it down and then wrap it in the plastic wrap. Place it in a large zippered plastic bag and freeze up to 1 month. Thaw in the fridge overnight. Let stand at room temperature for 40 minutes before shaping.

parm-dusted garlic-butter pull-apart dinner rolls

MAKES 18 ROLLS
ACTIVE TIME: 40 MINUTES
TOTAL TIME: 2 HOURS 10 MINUTES (INCLUDING DOUBLE RISING TIME)

All I can tell you is these rolls get hoovered up so fast they barely have time to cool. The super-fun method of forming the balls of dough by dragging them (YASS, DRAG THEM) under your cupped hand was something we picked up from a few baking books we read while we were making *this* book, so a thank you to pro bakers Melissa Weller and Claire Saffitz for helping us get our perfect roll on!

The dough balls rise into one another until they alllllmost touch, then bake into a tray full of kissing bread cousins (Why did I just write that??). The middles are stretchy-tender-fluffy-yeasty-doughy good, and the garlic and parm work super-well. I can see these being served with a perfect steak or roast chicken dinner, or warmed up the next morning to soak up bacon grease.

1½ sticks (12 tablespoons) very soft unsalted butter, plus more for buttering the pan and bowl

¾ teaspoon garlic salt

1 cup whole milk

2 tablespoons sugar

1 packet (2¼ teaspoons) active dry yeast

3⅔ cups flour, plus more as needed

2 eggs

1½ teaspoons fine sea salt

¼ cup (½ ounce) finely grated Parmigiano-Reggiano cheese

1 Measure 5 tablespoons of the butter into a small bowl and add the garlic salt. In a glass bowl, microwave the milk until it feels like just-warm bathwater, about 1 minute. Whisk in 1 tablespoon of the sugar and the yeast and stir until dissolved; let sit until a frothy disc of yeast forms in the center of the milk, 7 to 8 minutes.

2 In the bowl of a stand mixer fitted with the paddle attachment, combine 3⅓ cups of the flour with the frothy milk, 1 egg, and the remaining tablespoon sugar. Beat on low speed until a sticky but unified dough forms, 2 minutes. Add the salt and beat another minute, then gradually add the remaining 7 tablespoons butter and ⅓ cup flour. Mix until a soft but not super-sticky dough forms, 8 to 9 minutes. Transfer the dough to a lightly floured surface, grease it all over with a tiny bit of melted butter, return it to the bowl, cover tightly with plastic wrap, and let rise in a warm spot until doubled in size, about 1 hour.

3 Grease a glass 9 × 13-inch baking dish generously with butter. Uncover the dough, transfer to a clean work surface, and punch down a couple of times, folding the dough and turning 90 degrees after each punch. Divide the dough into 18 equal pieces, pinching the cut ends closed underneath. Flour your hands. One at a time, place a roll on the counter and cover it with a cupped, floured hand. Drag the roll toward you, pulling on the surface to tighten the roll, repeating 1 or 2 more times.

4 Arrange the rolls in the buttered pan in 3 rows of 6 each. Cover with a clean kitchen towel and let rise in a warm spot until the rolls rise again and spring back when pressed, 30 to 35 minutes. Beat the remaining egg in a bowl with a fork, then gently brush the rolls with the egg.

5 Preheat the oven to 350°F. Bake until the tops are shiny, dry, and deep brown, 22 to 23 minutes. During the last few minutes of baking, melt the garlic butter in the microwave for 15 seconds. When the rolls come out, brush them several times with butter and sprinkle with parm. Serve hot hot hot!

sesame parm soup—sticks

MAKES 20 STICKS
ACTIVE TIME: 20 MINUTES
TOTAL TIME: 1 HOUR 45 MINUTES
(INCLUDING SINGLE RISING TIME)

If you had the kind of year I had last year . . . oh, wait, you *did* have that kind of year. So, join me when I say: f*ck sourdough, f*ck kombucha, f*ck kimchi! Okay, they're fine, but I am pretty OVER crafty foods that take two weeks to get going. Soups were *our* culinary mascot, more often than not our entire meal. Which I am *completely* okay with, but after a while I felt a little bad for our poor soups, naked in their bowls with no companionship.

Enter these sticks, the perfect accessory for any one of the soups in the next chapter. They're the kind of thing you'd ordinarily buy, but since you prob have absolutely everything you need to throw them together and you've done enough macrame / knitting / tidying / scrapbooking / letterpressing to last you a lifetime, spend a few minutes to make these toasty, cheesy, crunchy breadsticks. Your soups will thank you.

⅔ cup warm water

1 teaspoon active dry yeast

1 teaspoon sugar

2¼ cups flour, plus more for dusting the surface

⅓ cup olive oil, plus more for brushing the breadsticks

¾ teaspoon fine sea salt, plus more for rolling the breadsticks

¼ teaspoon freshly ground black pepper

⅔ cup finely shredded Parmigiano-Reggiano cheese

¼ cup raw sesame seeds

1 In the bowl of a stand mixer, whisk together the warm water, yeast, and sugar and let the yeast bloom for 10 minutes. (You'll know it's working if it foams up.)

2 Add the 2¼ cups flour and ⅓ cup olive oil, attach the paddle (it works better here because there's not that much dough), and knead at medium-low speed until the dough comes together, 2 to 3 minutes. Add the ¾ teaspoon salt and ¼ teaspoon pepper and mix until the dough is soft but not sticky, 5 to 6 minutes, adding ¼ cup of the cheese during the last minute.

3 Cover the bowl with plastic wrap and let sit in a warm place until almost doubled in size, 45 minutes to 1 hour.

4 Preheat the oven to 425°F. Line 2 large baking sheets with parchment paper.

5 Lightly flour a work surface and scoop the dough out onto the surface. Divide the dough into 20 pieces. Use your hands to roll each piece into a 12- to 14-inch rope between ¼ and ½ inch thick. Toss the sesame seeds and remaining cheese on a sheet tray and roll the ropes in the mixture, pressing slightly to adhere. Arrange them on the prepared baking sheets, then brush them with olive oil and sprinkle with a little more salt. Bake until deep golden brown and crisp, 13 to 15 minutes, rotating the sheets midway. Let the breadsticks cool slightly, then stand up in glasses to cool completely. (Store the breadsticks in an airtight container for up to 5 days; if you wish, rewarm them in a 300°F oven for 10 minutes.)

uncle mike's focaccia

SERVES 10 TO 12
ACTIVE TIME: 30 MINUTES
TOTAL TIME: 28 HOURS
(DONE OVER 2 DAYS, WITH SEVERAL RISINGS)

There's something really special about a fluffy, airy, holey, slightly tangy focaccia. Luckily for us, our dear friend Mike Rosenthal, who usually just drops off bags and bags of it while it's still warm from his oven, actually came over one day and taught us how to make it.

Yes, it's definitely a weekend project. You kind of need to be around, and know how to use your cellphone's timer, to perfect it. But trust me, it's worth it. It's almost a meal in itself (I've made it one on more than one occasion), but it pairs well with almost anything—a little dipping plate of good olive oil and balsamic or sliced avocados—or could be used for a turkey sandwich. It's one of those breads that doesn't sit long enough to get old, it just disappears. Just make sure you hide some for yourself.

I know it seems just wayyyyy fussier than I would ever normally be to tell you to use a baking scale to weigh the ingredients, but that's the only way to get the amounts exactly as Uncle Mike gave them to us. But if you don't have one, you can measure with a cup. It might end up a little different, but it's yours! And no bread is better than *your* bread.

575 grams (about 4¼ cups) flour

475 grams (about 2 cups) room-temperature water

¾ teaspoon active dry yeast or ½ teaspoon instant yeast

12 grams (2 teaspoons) fine sea salt

4½ tablespoons olive oil, plus more for spreading the dough

½ cup firm small cherry tomatoes, halved

1 tablespoon finely chopped fresh rosemary

1½ teaspoons flaky sea salt, such as Maldon

1 In a medium bowl, combine 75 grams each of the flour (scant ½ cup) and water (⅓ cup) with the yeast. Cover tightly with plastic wrap and let it sit out at room temperature, at least 12 hours and up to 18 hours. The mixture, called the poolish or the pre-ferment, will be bubbling and smell very yeasty and sour!

2 After that 12- to 18-hour wait, place the salt and 75 grams (5 tablespoons) warm water in a small bowl and stir to let the salt dissolve. Combine the poolish with the remaining 500 grams (about 3¾ cups) flour and the remaining 325 grams (1 cup plus 6 tablespoons) water in a large, clean container with a lid (or one that you can wrap tightly with plastic) and stir with your hands until just combined and there are no lumps or dry patches.

3 Cover tightly and wait 30 minutes, then uncover and add the dissolved salt water and stir and squeeze the dough, using your hands again, until the water is fully incorporated. Cover tightly and set a timer for 30 minutes.

4 Uncover the dough and, using wet hands, gently scoop it up from one side and fold it over to the other. Repeat this fold 2 more times, starting from a new side of the dough. No need to mix or knead; you're just folding the dough over on itself from different angles. Reseal or recover the container, set the timer for another 30 minutes, then repeat the folding process. Reseal, set another timer, uncover, and repeat the folding process for a third time. If the dough appears very aerated and fluffy, you're ready to move on to the next step. If not, reseal, set the timer for 30 minutes, and let the dough rise one last time.

5 Generously brush 1½ tablespoons of the olive oil on the bottom and sides of a metal 9 x 13-inch brownie pan or other baking dish. Carefully turn the dough from the larger container into the dish, gently releasing it from the container but trying not to deflate the dough. Using lightly

oiled hands, very gently spread the dough out, cover with the lid (or a tightly sealed layer of plastic), and refrigerate for at least 12 hours, and up to 18 hours.

6 Unseal the dough gently, again being careful not to tear or deflate the dough, and let it warm up, uncovered, at room temperature for about 1 hour 30 minutes. Place a pizza stone in the oven and preheat the oven to 500°F. (If you don't have a pizza stone, place a heavy baking sheet in the oven during the last 20 minutes of preheating.)

7 Once the dough has warmed up, place the remaining

3 tablespoons olive oil in a small finger bowl. Dip a hand in the oil and begin to poke the dough with all 5 fingers all the way down to the bottom of the dough, repeating about 7 times to make about 35 holes. Poke a cherry tomato half, cut side up, as far down into each hole as you can, and scatter any remaining tomatoes evenly across the dough. Drizzle a little more olive oil evenly all over the dough and sprinkle with the rosemary and flaky salt.

8 Place the pan on the pizza stone or baking sheet and bake until parts of the bread are

deep golden brown and the bread is cooked through, about 15 minutes. Remove from the oven, and cool on your stovetop or a cooling rack for 15 to 20 minutes. Loosen the sides of the bread with a butter knife and lift it out onto a cutting board. Use a serrated knife to cut the focaccia into squares or slices.

9 If there is any left, cool the focaccia completely and store in an airtight container or wrapped in plastic wrap in the refrigerator, as the bread can mold quickly. Reheat on a baking sheet in a 400°F oven for 10 minutes.

sides + soup

crispy delicata squash chips

SERVES 4 (BUT REALLY 1; DON'T KID YOURSELF)
ACTIVE TIME: 10 MINUTES
TOTAL TIME: 35 MINUTES

We all know that weirdo squash display that shows up every October in your grocery store produce area. To be honest, I truly thought most of these . . . gourds . . . were used for fall doorstep decor, or to bring a little "meh, looks good" to the center of your dinner table. But no!!! And I cannot stress the "no!!!" enough!

The weird-looking dinosaur-egg–looking squashes with the dots and lines* make for an INCREDIBLE little squash chip. I know most people wouldn't use that word for something as boring-sounding as a squash chip, but let me tell you, I could not stop eating these. I mean, look, this entire book's creative process was basically Adeena and me making three to six recipes a day for months, then at the end we removed some recipes that just didn't fit in the vibe, no matter how good they were.

The fact that these squash chips knocked out *some really great* recipes should tell you how much faith I have in these being your perfect snack. The only thing is, they're best eaten superfresh, while they're still crisp.

*Oh, they're called Delicata squash. Deliciousata!

1 Preheat the oven to 425°F.

2 Trim the bottom and top of the squash, then halve the squash crosswise. Use a spoon to scrape around the inside of the squash halves, hollowing them out so they look like tubes. Use a sharp knife to slice them into ¼-inch-thin rings, or even thinner if you want the crispiest rounds.

3 Toss the squash in a bowl with the olive oil and season generously with salt and pepper. Arrange in a single layer on a rimmed baking sheet and roast, flipping once, until some are deeply golden and crisp on both sides and some are a little softer in places, 18 to 24 minutes total. Taste, season with more salt and pepper if needed, and dust with the parm.

1 large or 2 small Delicata squash (about 1 pound total)

3 tablespoons olive oil

Kosher salt and freshly ground black pepper

Finely grated Parmigiano-Reggiano cheese

whole-roasted oyster mushrooms

SERVES 2 TO 3
ACTIVE TIME: 3 MINUTES
TOTAL TIME: 18 MINUTES

Not gonna lie, I had never encountered this kind of mushroom before I started getting a weekly box from my friends at Flamingo Farms, a most beautiful place with a gorgeous kitchen and the kindest owners in the world. We once called to ask if we could do a picnic on the grounds, assuming it was a public spot, but in fact it was just them and . . . their house. But they let us do it. They even let Pepper cook on premises!

So. Back to those 'shrooms. They're called oysters because they sort of look like them, growing in big petals. They have the most amazing ability to get crisp when roasted. If you are lucky and get whole heads (or bunches, or clumps? I don't know the technical term, but a lot of them stuck together) from specialty shroomists (yes, I definitely made that word up), you can roast these babies until they're crispy *and* juicy, and you will never. miss. meat. again. No, I'm not going vegan, but these could hold me over for a good, long while. If you can't find the whole ones, you can more easily find them already separated into velvety mushroom petals, equally delicious when crisped.

1 Preheat the oven to 500°F. During the last 10 minutes of preheating, place a small rimmed baking sheet or square baking dish in the oven to preheat. When the oven is preheated, use an oven mitt to remove the sheet from the oven, drizzle 1½ tablespoons of the oil on the baking sheet, arrange the mushrooms on the baking sheet, and drizzle all over with the remaining 1½ tablespoons oil.

2 Season with the salt and pepper and return the sheet to the oven. Roast until the mushrooms wilt slightly, look shiny from releasing some of their juices, and the edges are dry and charred, 13 to 18 minutes.

3 tablespoons olive oil

1 head (1 pound) fresh oyster mushrooms, or 1 pound packaged mushroom pieces, tough stems removed*

1 teaspoon kosher salt

½ teaspoon freshly ground black pepper

*If using the mushroom pieces, toss them with the oil, salt, and pepper in a bowl first, and then spread them out on the baking sheet and roast until crispy and golden, 12 to 13 minutes. (Keep an eye and nose on them, though, a few minutes before—don't let them burn!)

arti-chokes

with hot garlicky melted butter

SERVES 4
ACTIVE TIME: 15 MINUTES
TOTAL TIME: 1 HOUR

Steamed artichokes! Oh my goodness, you make these once and you will never stop because the dirty little secret is how laughably easy they are to prepare. Fun to eat, too—once they're cooked in their lemony garlicky broth, you get to pluck off individual petals from the artichoke, dip them in garlic butter (or mayo, or Wishbone, or anything else you want!), then scrape the luscious veggie velvet off with your teeth before discarding the leaf and starting all over again . . . and then you get to the meaty heart and go to town.

They're first-course dinner party-worthy, but also a perfect sort of light lunch kind of a meal that will satisfy you without weighing you down.

4 large artichokes

1 lemon

½ cup dry white wine (optional)

1 dried bay leaf

10 whole black peppercorns

5 garlic cloves

1 stick (8 tablespoons) unsalted butter

2 teaspoons Sriracha or Cholula hot sauce, plus more to taste

¼ teaspoon kosher salt, plus more for seasoning

Left-leaning artichoke!

1 Make sure you have a steamer basket that fits into a pot (a metal colander also works) that has a tight-fitting lid.

2 Place an artichoke on a cutting board and trim off the top ½ inch with a sharp knife. Peel off and discard any loose, dried bottom leaves. Use scissors to trim just the thorny tips off the remaining leaves. Repeat with the remaining artichokes.

3 Halve the lemon, then cut one half into thin semi-rounds and the other half into 4 wedges. Place the lemon slices in the pot and add about 2 cups of water along with the wine (if using), bay leaf, peppercorns, and 2 of the garlic cloves. Place the steamer basket in the pot; it's okay if the liquid comes up into the basket a bit.

Bring the liquid to a boil over high heat, then add the artichokes to the steamer basket, reduce the heat to low, cover, and steam until the artichokes are tender and a leaf pulls off easily from the inner part of the artichoke, 40 to 45 minutes.

4 During the last 10 minutes of the steaming, warm the butter in a small saucepan over medium-low heat, stirring occasionally, until melted. Mince the remaining 3 garlic cloves and add to the butter; cook, stirring often, until fragrant and the garlic has softened, 3 or 4 minutes. Remove from the heat, stir in the 2 teaspoons hot sauce and ¼ teaspoon salt, and cover to keep warm.

5 Remove the artichokes from the steamer. Uncover and whisk the butter until well blended, and serve each artichoke with 2 tablespoons of the garlic butter and a lemon wedge.

6 To eat the artichokes, pull off individual leaves and scrape the meaty flesh off the bottom with your teeth. Once you get to the artichoke center, pull off the more papery leaves surrounding the choke (the hairy, fuzzy part) and remove the choke with a spoon, making sure to reserve the artichoke heart sitting just beneath. Savor that heart and stem!

parmesan whipped mashed pota—toes

SERVES 6 TO 8
ACTIVE TIME: 20 MINUTES
TOTAL TIME: 40 MINUTES

Every cook has a personal arsenal—recipes that you pretty much know how to make anytime. Things like roasted chicken, tomato soup, Mom's Thai chili sauce, pancakes . . . stuff that just makes your life work.

But no matter what else is in your arsenal, mashed potatoes are a must, a component of a meal that binds everything together—the main, the sauce, the sides. It never, ever make things worse, only better. (I lived in Idaho when I was a kid.)

And they're truly hard to f*ck up. I've only done that once in my life, and even that is more than most people. That time, I let the potatoes boil until soft, then turned the heat off and let them sit in the hot water long enough to create potato glue when I mashed them. I honestly have never seen anything like it—they were just complete starchy glue. But you know what? The flavor was still incredible.* It was like . . . if you love eating glue, this dish is a dream? I dunno.

Anyway, this recipe is for buttery mashed potatoes that are light and fluffy, whipped with the flavor of sharp Parmigiano. Yes, it makes a lot, but you can halve it . . . and who doesn't want *more* mashed potatoes? These can be eaten with about 80 percent of the dishes in the book or simply eaten alone while watching *Peaky Blinders* start to finish, like me. Did you know it's pronounced kill-ian?

*Okay, the other way you can eff them up is by making them in a blender or food processor, which also turns them into glue. Don't do that! Unless you *want* to.

4 pounds (8 medium) russet or Yukon Gold potatoes (or a combination)

½ cup heavy cream

1 stick (8 tablespoons) unsalted butter, plus more for topping

1 tablespoon kosher salt, plus more for seasoning

2 ounces Parmigiano-Reggiano cheese, finely grated (1 cup), plus more for topping

3 tablespoons finely minced fresh chives

1 Peel and cut the potatoes into 1½-inch pieces. Place the potatoes in a large pot, cover with 3 inches of water, and bring to a boil over high heat. Reduce the heat to medium-low to maintain a vigorous simmer and cook, uncovered, until the potatoes can easily be pierced with a wooden skewer or a dinner knife, 15 to 20 minutes.

2 While the potatoes are cooking, warm the cream and butter in a small bowl in the microwave until the butter is just melted, 30 seconds to 1 minute. When the potatoes are done, drain and place them in a stand mixer fitted with the whisk attachment (or use a handheld mixer and large bowl). Add the cream-butter mixture, the 1 tablespoon salt, and the 1 cup cheese. Starting on low speed, whip the potatoes, gradually increasing the speed to high and whipping until fluffy, 30 to 45 seconds (much more, and the potatoes could get gluey!).

3 Season with more salt to taste, transfer to a serving bowl, dot with pats of butter, dust with some more parm, and garnish with the chives. Serve immediately. (If the potatoes cool down and start to stiffen, warm a bit of cream in a small saucepan or the microwave, drizzle it in, and whip again with a whisk.)

salt-roasted yams

with lime-yogurt sauce, pine nuts & hot honey

SERVES 2
ACTIVE TIME: 20 MINUTES
TOTAL TIME: 1 HOUR 30 MINUTES

I'm not sure I've ever seen a dish that looked as perfect as it tasted. To me, usually the sloppiest-looking meals taste the absolute best, but this? Not this one. This roasted, crispy-skinned sweet potato is home to a creamy, lime-infused yogurt, and every single bite pops with honey, garlic, and the crunch of toasted pine nuts. I have no idea why, but these flavors were meant to be together. And while, yes, it is a potato, and a potato screams side piece, I definitely say this should be the one and only for your dinner plate tonight.

1 cup kosher salt,* plus more for seasoning

2 large sweet potatoes (the orange things we sometimes call yams)

¼ cup honey

½ teaspoon red pepper flakes

1 lime

⅔ cup plain whole-milk yogurt

3 tablespoons olive oil

¼ cup pine nuts

4 garlic cloves, minced

Cilantro leaves, for garnish

*The salt helps caramelize the bottom of the potato more evenly, but if you don't have that much extra kosher salt or don't feel like using it, just roast the taters directly on the baking sheet.

1 Preheat the oven to 425°F. Arrange the 1 cup salt in a small sheet pan or rimmed baking sheet to act as a stand / cushion, then arrange the sweet potatoes on top of the salt. Roast the potatoes until the skin looks tight and puffy and the flesh is soft, 1 hour (or longer, if needed).

2 While the potatoes are roasting, combine the honey and red pepper flakes in a small microwave-safe bowl and microwave just until warm, 10 to 15 seconds. Remove from the oven and let come to room temperature.

3 Halve the lime. Cut one half of the lime into 2 wedges and reserve. Zest the other half with a microplane into the yogurt, then squeeze in 1 teaspoon of the juice (save the rest of that half for another use). Add some salt to taste, cover, and chill until ready to use.

4 In a medium skillet, warm the olive oil over medium heat. Add the pine nuts and toast them, shaking the pan, until the nuts begin to darken slightly, 4 to 5 minutes. Reduce the heat to medium-low, then add the garlic and cook, stirring, until the garlic is lightly golden and some of the pieces are a tiny bit crisp, another 2 to 3 minutes. Remove from the stove and cover to keep warm.

5 When the sweet potatoes are cooked, split them horizontally and return them to the oven, flesh side up, until the edges crisp slightly, another 10 to 15 minutes.

6 Remove the sweet potatoes from the oven, brushing the salt off the bottoms. Arrange the sweet potatoes on a platter and dollop some of the yogurt mixture inside each potato half. Spoon some of the pine nut topping on top of the yogurt, sprinkle with the cilantro, then drizzle some of the spicy honey on top of each potato half. Serve with the lime wedges.

tangy
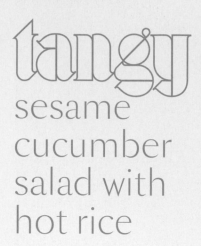

sesame cucumber salad with hot rice

SERVES 4
ACTIVE TIME: 15 MINUTES
TOTAL TIME: 45 MINUTES (INCLUDING SALTING TIME)

I can be a bit of a perfectionist when it comes to making recipes for you. If it isn't 10/10, it's trash to me, which is why sometimes if something isn't jussssst so, I'll just dial-in an order of McNuggets and fries and call it a night. But in the case of this cucumber salad, I persevered (cue inspirational music). I pushed through, because the world deserves more than another watery cuke salad that releases all its liquid into your painstakingly crafted dressing, diluting the flavors and your hopes and dreams.

So, I took the extra time to salt and drain the cucumber slices, and even a little longer to pat them dry, so that instead of a veggie swimming pool in a bowl, you get a little bit of sweet, sesame, spicy, funky, and crunchy in every bite. We have a fresh batch of rice-cooker rice on at all times (thanks, Mom), and so the spirit moved me to pile the salad on top of a scoop of hot carbs, and the hot-cool, crunchy-soft contrast really did it for me. Is it a weird meal? Maybe! But this is the best part of cooking at home—just make yourself happy, no rules needed or heeded. There were no McNuggets that night! (But now that I think about it, they would go together . . .)

1 In a large bowl, toss the cucumbers with the salt, then transfer them to a fine-mesh strainer set over a bowl and drain the cucumbers until about ¼ cup greenish liquid ends up in the bowl, about 30 minutes.

2 Discard the liquid, then arrange the cucumbers on a single layer of paper towels. Top with another layer of paper towels, then press down to remove any excess liquid.

3 In a jar, combine the oil, vinegar, sugar, fish sauce, and sesame oil. Seal tightly, and shake until the dressing is creamy. Return the cucumbers to the bowl along with the avocado, scallions, and jalapeño, then add the dressing to the cucumbers and very gently toss.

4 If serving with rice, you can either mound the rice in the center of a large plate, scatter the salad around it, then drizzle with the salad and dressing; or mound the rice in individual bowls and divide the salad and dressing among the bowls. Garnish with the sesame seeds and cilantro, and serve.

1 pound Persian cucumbers, thinly sliced

2 teaspoons kosher salt

6 tablespoons peanut or vegetable oil

2 tablespoons rice vinegar

5 teaspoons sugar

2½ teaspoons fish sauce

2 teaspoons toasted sesame oil

1 small avocado, cut into ⅛-inch-thick slices

¼ cup thinly sliced scallion greens

1 small jalapeño pepper (preferably red), minced

2 cups hot cooked rice, for serving (if you're into it)

1 tablespoon toasted sesame seeds

Fresh cilantro leaves, for garnish

Lol

broccoli salad
with creamy cashew dressing

SERVES 4
ACTIVE TIME: 20 MINUTES
TOTAL TIME: 25 MINUTES

Have you ever ordered an entire huge takeout order just because you wanted one teeny tiny item? I definitely went through that phase with Sweetgreen, when I was ordering salads just so I could get to the plastic cup of cashew dressing that came with them. I would try (and fail) to not sound weird, putting "WILL TIP BIG FOR EXTRA DRESSING" in the order notes.

Well, here is my take on that blessed dressing, and the ideal salad to go underneath it. The bright green broccoli is begging to be picked up by hand and swiped through the dressing-soaked plate, or you can be a grownup and knife-and-fork it to get all the little bits of cranberry, red onion, and toasted nuts. You might just want to double the dressing. You're welcome—no tip necessary!

2 medium heads of broccoli (about 1½ pounds total), trimmed and separated into florets (6 cups florets)

Kosher salt

1 cup chopped salted roasted cashews

3 garlic cloves, smashed

½ teaspoon toasted sesame oil

2 tablespoons unseasoned rice vinegar

1½ tablespoons sugar

1 teaspoon finely diced jalapeño pepper (preferably red, with seeds)

2 teaspoons light soy sauce

1 teaspoon fish sauce

¼ cup thinly sliced red onion

¼ cup sweetened dried cranberries (such as Craisins)

1 Place about 1¼ cups of water in a 5-quart saucepan and bring to a boil over high heat. Add the broccoli, cover with a tight-fitting lid, and steam until the broccoli turns bright green but is still tender-crisp, 3 minutes. Drain if there is any water left, then spread the broccoli in a single layer on a paper towel–lined tray to cool for 10 minutes (don't submerge in cold water because it will make the broccoli soggy). Season the broccoli to taste with salt. If you like your broccoli salad cold, transfer to a bowl and chill for 30 minutes.

2 While the broccoli is cooling, make the dressing: Combine ⅔ cup of the cashews with the ⅓ cup water, garlic, sesame oil, vinegar, sugar, jalapeño, soy sauce, and fish sauce in a blender and blend until smooth and creamy, 1 minute; add water by the teaspoon if the dressing is too thick.

3 Arrange the broccoli on a platter, then scatter the onions and cranberries on top. Drizzle ½ cup of the dressing over the broccoli, then scatter the remaining ⅓ cup cashews over the salad. Serve the remaining dressing on the side.

jon & vinny's cornmeal fried scallions

with chrissy's pepperoncini cilantro sauce

SERVES 4
ACTIVE TIME: 25 MINUTES
TOTAL TIME: 30 MINUTES

It's truly incredible and beautiful that, despite the fact that everyone knows about it, Jon & Vinny's, a little Italian restaurant nestled amid all the sneakerhead shops on Fairfax Avenue in Los Angeles, still feels like a secret spot. I have friends that have had a standing Sunday-night reservation there since the early days. People are diehards! (Of course, the chef/owners, Jon Shook and Vinny Dotolo, have won every award there is to win, but they really made it in my eyes when they got to do an airplane menu! Basically, that's my lifelong goal/dream [see page 217], and they grabbed that brass ring. But I digress.) Back to the restaurant. Every single thing on the menu is good; my favorite is the six-hour bolognese, John loves the cacio e pepe . . . the list goes on and on. I saw this scallion creation on the menu just once, but I've wanted to make it at home forever. Because Jon and Vinny are the greatest, they gave us the recipe! You batter and deep-fry long scallion strands, then munch on them like a rabbit.

The bottom parts are superoniony and flavorful, and the green tops cling to the cornmeally batter. Crunch a munch! To go with it we made a spicy two-minute sauce that's the perfect balance for the deep-fried richness.

Bonus: When you serve this to friends, it's pretty much guaranteed to be their first time eating it—and how often can you say that these days? Make this, then praise the gods that are Jon and Vinny.

Sauce

½ cup jarred sliced pepperoncini, drained

½ cup (packed) fresh cilantro leaves

½ cup olive oil

1 large garlic clove

¼ teaspoon kosher salt

Scallions

Vegetable oil, for deep-frying

2 cups flour

1½ cups coarse cornmeal or polenta

2 teaspoons onion powder

1½ teaspoons garlic powder

1 tablespoon kosher salt, plus more for seasoning

2½ cups cold buttermilk

3 bunches scallions

1 MAKE THE SAUCE: Combine the pepperoncini, cilantro, olive oil, garlic, and salt in a bullet-style or other high-powered blender, or in the small bowl of a food processor, and blend until smooth, 15 seconds (or use an immersion blender!).

2 MAKE THE SCALLIONS: Fill a large, high-sided skillet suitable for deep-frying about halfway with vegetable oil and gently warm over medium heat to 350°F (use a candy or deep-fry thermometer if you have one). Reduce the heat to medium-low to maintain the temperature if you need more time to prep the scallions.

3 In a 9 × 13-inch baking dish, combine the flour, cornmeal, onion powder, garlic powder, and 1 tablespoon salt. Place the buttermilk in another 9 × 13-inch baking dish.

4 Cut the furry ends (roots) off the scallions and trim any raggedy green ends. Use a sharp paring knife to score both ends of the scallions lengthwise 4 to 6 times (cutting 2 to 3 inches on each side) so they still hold together in the middle but have a frizzled look.

5 Working in batches, dip the scored scallions into the buttermilk, then lift them out and let the excess drip off. Then dip them into the cornmeal, pressing to let it adhere. Transfer the coated scallions to a parchment-lined baking sheet.

6 Return the heat to medium, if necessary. Working with a few at a time, lower the scallions into the oil and fry, bending the scallions a bit to make different shapes and adjusting the oil temperature up or down to keep it at around 350°F. Fry the scallions until golden and crispy, 3 to 4 minutes total, flipping them midway through. Drain on paper towels, then season with salt and serve with the sauce.

a really great salad
with lots of options

SERVES 4
ACTIVE TIME: 15 MINUTES
TOTAL TIME: 30 MINUTES (INCLUDING CHILLING TIME)

This salad started out in one place and ended up in another because *someone* was on a campaign to make me like beets, and she almost succeeded—but almost just wasn't good enough. (Try again next book, Sussman.) I'm sure those dirty roasted roots would please many of you, but this mix-and-match salad will please *all* of you.

So, select the lettuce you love, the fruit you desire, the nuts you crave, the cheese you please. All I ask is that you make the creamy balsamic dressing to the letter, because it truly goes with everything and will make you look good (and your salad taste good) no matter what combination you go with.

Nuts

½ cup shelled raw pistachios (or any nuts you love)

2 tablespoons sugar

2 tablespoons unsalted butter

⅛ teaspoon kosher salt, plus more for seasoning

Generous pinches of freshly ground black pepper

Cayenne pepper

Creamy Balsamic Dressing

3 tablespoons balsamic vinegar

2 teaspoons grainy Dijon mustard

1 tablespoon water

½ teaspoon kosher salt

¼ teaspoon freshly ground black pepper

½ cup olive oil

Salad

¼ cup thinly sliced red onion

5 cups (about 5 ounces) baby Gem lettuce (or any lettuce of your choice), leaves separated

6 ripe figs, quartered (or 1 medium pear, 2 plums, or any fruit of your choice, really, thinly sliced)

½ (5.2-ounce) package Boursin Garlic & Fine Herbs cheese (or 2½ ounces any goat cheese), crumbled (about ⅓ cup)

Freshly cracked black peppercorns

1 MAKE THE NUTS: Combine the pistachios, sugar, butter, ⅛ teaspoon salt, and the black pepper in a medium nonstick skillet and cook, stirring constantly, over medium heat, until the sugar melts, coats the nuts, darkens slightly, and smells nutty, 4 to 5 minutes. Transfer to a plate, sprinkle with the cayenne, cool completely (about 10 minutes), then break apart. Season with more salt, pepper, or cayenne, if desired.

2 MAKE THE DRESSING: Combine the vinegar, mustard, water, salt, and pepper in a medium bowl. Slowly drizzle in the olive oil, whisking as you drizzle, until the dressing gets thick and creamy.

3 ASSEMBLE THE SALAD: If desired, place the onion in a bowl, cover with ice water for 10 minutes, then drain and pat dry (this makes the onion a little less pungent and keeps it crisp). Combine the lettuce, figs, and onion on a serving platter. Scatter the cheese and nuts on top, drizzle with half of the dressing, and top with lots of cracked black peppercorns. Serve the remaining dressing on the side or reserve for another use.

Cous-cous salad
with apricot basil dressing

SERVES 6 TO 8
ACTIVE TIME: 15 MINUTES
TOTAL TIME: 25 MINUTES

We originally made this with boxed Moroccan-style couscous, but during the photo shoot, our stylists accidentally swapped in Israeli couscous and the recipe came out even better than the original! Also known as pearl couscous, Israeli couscous is actually made up of tiny pasta balls, similar to Italian fregola, and just super-great in pasta salads. Once you boil the Israeli couscous, you're ready to add a jillion things, turning it into a tasty ladies' lunch with leftovers. Here, we load it up with herbs, nuts, dried fruits, and chickpeas, but a can of tuna, cubes of cheese, or ribbons of smoked turkey would be more than welcome if you wanted that instead.

½ cup dried apricots

¼ cup boiling water

1 teaspoon kosher salt, plus more for seasoning

2 cups Israeli couscous

½ cup plus 1 tablespoon olive oil

¼ cup white wine vinegar

¾ cup (packed) fresh basil leaves, plus more for garnish

1 tablespoon honey

2 teaspoons Dijon mustard

2 garlic cloves

1 (15-ounce) can chickpeas, drained and rinsed

½ cup chopped dried cherries

½ cup plus 2 tablespoons toasted sliced almonds

1 Finely chop the apricots, then place half of them in a bowl, cover with the boiling water, and let sit until the water is absorbed, about 15 minutes. Drain off any remaining water.

2 While the apricots are soaking, bring half a pot of generously salted water to a boil. Add the couscous, return to a boil, and cook until al dente, 7 to 8 minutes. Drain, rinse briefly under cold water, drain again, then transfer to a large bowl and toss with 1 tablespoon of the olive oil to prevent it from sticking.

3 Combine the soaked apricots in a blender with ½ cup olive oil, the vinegar, ¼ cup of the basil, the honey, mustard, and garlic. Add 1 teaspoon salt and blend until smooth, 30 seconds.

4 Thinly slice the remaining ½ cup basil leaves and add to the bowl with the couscous along with the chickpeas, dried cherries, ½ cup of the toasted almonds, and the remaining ¼ cup apricots. Toss with the dressing, season with more salt to taste, and top with the remaining 2 tablespoons almonds.

citrus & burrata
caprese

SERVES 6
ACTIVE TIME: 30 MINUTES
TOTAL TIME: 30 MINUTES

Living in California in the winter has its advantages, among them an incredible winter crop of citrus *and* tomatoes at the same time. We put them all together for this totally gorgeous salad that I would be pretty happy consuming all by myself for lunch. But it's also great to share!

Even if you don't live in California, these days you can get good grape or hothouse tomatoes in the winter and citrus from South America in the summer. Just make sure to take the burrata out of the fridge for a while before serving, so its center can do the full ooze and gain you legions of new TikTok followers.

1 large or 2 medium balls burrata cheese (10–12 ounces total)

1½ pounds citrus fruit of your choice (blood oranges, tangerines, clementines, oranges, pink grapefruits), plus one more fruit for juice

3 tablespoons balsamic vinegar

1 teaspoon honey

1 teaspoon Dijon mustard

¼ teaspoon kosher salt, plus more for seasoning

¼ teaspoon freshly ground black pepper, plus more for seasoning

⅓ cup olive oil

¾ pound (2 medium) ripe multicolored heirloom or vine-ripened other tomatoes, cut into wedges

¼ cup shredded fresh basil

1 small jalapeño pepper, thinly sliced

1 Take the burrata out of the fridge and let it warm up a bit.

2 Cut the tops and bottoms off the citrus. Working from the top and using a sharp knife, follow the shape of the fruit and cut off strips of the peel and white pith, exposing the flesh but cutting off as little flesh as you need to. Work around the fruit, trimming here and there to remove any white stuff. (Don't throw away the rinds!)

3 Cut the fruit into ¼-inch-thick rounds. Squeeze all the juice from the rinds into a measuring cup; you should have ¼ to ⅓ cup; if you have less, supplement by squeezing an extra fruit to reach ⅓ cup. Pour the juice into a bowl, then whisk in the vinegar, honey, mustard, ¼ teaspoon salt, and ¼ teaspoon pepper. Drizzle in the olive oil in a steady stream, whisking constantly, until the dressing is smooth.

4 Remove the burrata from any liquid it's in, and gently pat it dry on a paper towel or clean dish towel. Arrange the burrata in the center of a serving platter, then surround it with the citrus and tomatoes. Scatter the basil and jalapeño all over the salad, then cut open the burrata and drizzle the dressing directly over the cheese; it will cover the plate underneath the citrus so you don't ruin the gorgeous look of the fruit. Season the salad to taste with additional salt and pepper.

creamed spinach stuffed mush-rooms

SERVES 3 TO 4
ACTIVE TIME: 25 MINUTES
TOTAL TIME: 40 MINUTES

You know how, when you're at a steakhouse, you think to yourself, "I should have some vegetables to go with this enormous slab of meat." And you see "creamed spinach" on the menu, and you go, "Yeah, spinach." You completely ignore the fact that you really just ordered a dish of hot cream, and when it lands, it feels damn good. Now, imagine if you took that creamed spinach and baked it until it's bubbling away inside seasoned mushrooms. You added another vegetable, so it feels *even better*!!

1 (10-ounce) package frozen chopped spinach, fully defrosted

2 tablespoons unsalted butter

1 small yellow onion, finely diced

1 tablespoon minced garlic

¼ teaspoon cayenne pepper

¾ cup heavy cream

1 tablespoon finely minced jalapeño (seeding optional)

1½ teaspoons kosher salt

⅛ teaspoon grated nutmeg

⅔ cup (3 ounces) shredded sharp cheddar cheese

⅔ cup (3 ounces) shredded pepper jack cheese

2 tablespoons plain dry bread crumbs

12 large (about 2-inch diameter) mushrooms (about ¾ pound), stems removed

1 tablespoon olive oil

1 Preheat the oven to 400°F and fit a wire rack in a foil-lined rimmed baking sheet.

2 Use your hands to squeeze the excess liquid thoroughly from the spinach. In a 9-inch skillet over medium heat, melt the butter, then add the onion and cook, stirring, until lightly golden, 7 to 8 minutes. Add the garlic and cayenne, and cook, stirring, 1 more minute. Add the spinach, cream, jalapeño, ½ teaspoon salt, and the nutmeg to the skillet and cook, stirring, until the mixture thickens, 2 minutes.

3 Remove the spinach mixture from the heat, transfer to a bowl, and stir in ½ cup each cheddar and pepper jack cheeses, along with the bread crumbs and ½ teaspoon salt.

4 Brush the outsides of the mushrooms with the olive oil, season the insides with the remaining ½ teaspoon salt, and fill each one with about 2 tablespoons of the filling (they will be piled high). Space the mushrooms out on the rack, leaving some room between each, and sprinkle each one with a generous teaspoon of the cheeses. Bake until the mushrooms are soft and the cheese is bubbling, 12 to 13 minutes.

wilted kale

with apples & bacon

SERVES 3 TO 4
ACTIVE TIME: 20 MINUTES
TOTAL TIME: 20 MINUTES

You'll be happy to see that I added bacon to kale because they work perfectly together. And bacon is happy because, bacon—which may have appeared in more recipes than any other ingredient except butter in my previous books—has been feeling neglected around here. Welcome back, BB!

2 slices bacon, chopped

3 garlic cloves, thinly sliced

1 small apple, cored, quartered, and thinly sliced

¼ teaspoon red pepper flakes

¾ cup low-sodium chicken broth

Kosher salt and freshly ground black pepper

½ pound dinosaur (lacinato) kale, stems discarded, leaves halved

Olive oil, for drizzling

1 Heat a heavy 9- or 10-inch skillet over medium-high heat until hot. Add the bacon and cook until crisped and the fat is rendered, 3 minutes. Tilt the pan to send the fat to one side, then scoop out the bacon onto a plate.

2 Reduce the heat to medium-low, then add the garlic and cook until just golden, 1 minute. Add the apple and red pepper flakes, raise the heat to medium, then cook, adding about ¼ cup chicken broth as you go, until the apple softens, 3 to 4 minutes.

3 Season lightly with salt and pepper, then add half the kale and about ¼ cup more chicken broth. Cook, stirring, until the kale wilts and turns bright green, then add the rest of the kale and remaining ¼ cup chicken broth and cook until all the kale is tender but still has some life, 3 to 4 minutes total. Season to taste with more salt and pepper, then transfer to a serving bowl, top with the bacon, and drizzle with some olive oil.

Note: For extra pork-on-pork action, serve this with the pork tenderloins on page 157 for an amazing meal.

veggie & shirataki noodles
with yolky broth

SERVES 6
ACTIVE TIME: 30 MINUTES
TOTAL TIME: 50 MINUTES

You probably know that I don't do diets. But what I *will* do is eat something cleanish when my body tells me it's time for a break from late-night hot pockets and sour sticks (these breaks are short-lived, but they are real). Still, I would only eat such a thing if I would eat it WITH a hot pocket and it could hold its own. Otherwise, why bother?

I actually love these slippery shirataki noodles, which are made from plants and are high-fiber/low-carb, but give you pasta vibes (they are refrigerated in the store near the tofu and stuff). Pile them with all the fresh veggies into a super-umami broth, thanks to our little friend MSG, who is finally coming out of the shadows to take her rightful moment in the sun (imagine being responsible for all the flavor of the world and having to hide just because of some myth about you being unhealthy! Every scientific study says it is NOT bad for you). Top this with a soft-boiled egg. Make a meal of it. The hot pockets can wait.

*If you can't find MSG, pop into your local Chinese restaurant and make a deal—a buck for a few tablespoons that will go a long way at home! Or . . . you know what? I guarantee you can find MSG in your grocery store. It's just called "Accent." It comes in a little shaker, and people have been buying it for DECADES, but didn't realize it was just MSG all along.

**A julienne peeler, available everywhere online, is the perfect tool for cutting thin strips of these veggies. If you don't have one, just use a regular peeler or a knife.

1 (8-ounce) package shirataki noodles (fettuccine or thin style), or other fresh cooked Asian-style noodles

8 cups low-sodium vegetable broth

1 teaspoon very finely minced fresh ginger (from about ½-inch piece)

2 garlic cloves, very thinly sliced

3 to 4 teaspoons kosher salt

1 tablespoon soy sauce (or 2 tablespoons low-sodium soy sauce)

1½ teaspoons toasted sesame oil, plus more for seasoning

½ teaspoon MSG* (or ½ vegetable bouillon cube)

1 medium zucchini, cut into thin strips**

1 medium yellow summer squash, cut into thin strips

1 small English cucumber, seedless part peeled and cut into thin strips

1 medium carrot, cut into thin strips

½ red bell pepper, cut into thin strips

1 small jalapeño pepper, very finely minced

1 cup shredded fresh basil

4 (6-minute) cooked eggs (see Note, page 107)

2 radishes, very thinly sliced into matchsticks

Hot chili oil and soy sauce, for garnish

RECIPE CONTINUES

1 Place the shirataki noodles in a colander and rinse with cold water for 1 minute; drain. (If you're using another kind of noodle, cook it according to package directions and rinse with cold water and drain.)

2 Place the broth, ginger, and garlic in a medium (at least 4-quart) saucepan and cook over medium heat until just simmering. Add 3 teaspoons of the salt, 1 tablespoon soy sauce, the sesame oil, and MSG and simmer 5 minutes. Drop in the zucchini, squash, cucumber, carrot, bell pepper, and jalapeño, reduce the heat to medium-low, and warm through for 10 minutes. Season to taste with more salt.

3 Stir in ½ cup of the basil and add the noodles to the serving bowls. Divide the broth among the bowls, then top each bowl with an egg and garnish with some more basil and the radishes. Let everyone season their bowl with more basil, soy sauce, and hot chili oil, as desired.

Perfect Six-Minute Eggs

Fill a medium saucepan with 1½ inches of water. Bring to a boil, then gently lower the eggs into the water with a slotted spoon. Return to a boil, cover, and cook exactly 6 minutes. (Use your phone timer!) Uncover and lift the eggs out into an ice-water bath to chill for 30 seconds. Gently peel.

greek-style
lemon, rice & chicken soup (avgolemono)

SERVES 6 TO 8
ACTIVE TIME: 30 MINUTES
TOTAL TIME: 1 HOUR

When does a food phase become a way of life? 'Cuz lately, I can't get enough of all things Greek. (I think my former feta aversion had influenced my POV on the whole Greek cuisine situation, but I've come around in the most obsessed way.) I even convinced (okay, begged) one of my closest friends to acquire one of my favorite pasta dishes, *pastitsio*, while she was in Greece, and smuggle it to me, still fresh, into Mexico.

Anyway, I digress. Avgolemono. Kind of the national soup of Greece. It's a chicken soup that's lemony, lush, perfect. You would be convinced that this velvety soup contained dairy because it's so incredibly creamy, but it's all thanks to eggs, which you just whisk into the broth to create a texture that never fails to amaze me. The rice's starch adds even *more* creaminess. I was going to make adding the pulled chicken breast optional, but it was so delicious it became mandatory before we even finished writing this recipe down.

1 COOK THE CHICKEN: Combine the garlic, 1 tablespoon of the olive oil, the salt, and the pepper in a small bowl, then rub the mixture all over the chicken. Heat the remaining 2 tablespoons olive oil in a 9- or 10-inch lidded skillet over medium-high heat. Add the chicken to the skillet and cook, trying not to move it, until golden on the bottom, about 5 minutes.

2 Reduce the heat to medium, carefully add ¼ cup of the chicken broth, quickly cover the skillet, and cook another 5 minutes. Uncover, flip the chicken, add the remaining ¼ cup broth, cover again, and cook until the chicken is white all the way through when cut, about another 5 minutes.

3 Remove from the heat and let cool, uncovered, until easy to handle. Using 2 forks, shred the chicken right in the skillet with its juices and cover to keep warm.

4 MAKE THE SOUP: Heat the olive oil over medium-low heat in a 4-quart Dutch oven. Add the onion and celery and cook, stirring occasionally, until the onion is soft and very lightly golden (you don't want dark edges here), 9 to 10 minutes. Add the garlic and cook, stirring, 1 additional minute.

Chicken

2 garlic cloves, finely minced

3 tablespoons olive oil

½ teaspoon kosher salt

¼ teaspoon freshly ground black pepper, plus more for garnish

2 skinless boneless chicken breasts (about 1 pound total)

½ cup low-sodium chicken broth (or taken from the 8 cups for the soup)

Soup

2 tablespoons olive oil

1 large onion, finely minced

1 celery stalk, finely minced

3 garlic cloves, minced

8 cups low-sodium chicken broth

1 teaspoon kosher salt

½ cup long-grain white rice

5 eggs

5 tablespoons fresh lemon juice

1 teaspoon chopped fresh oregano

Chopped fresh dill, for garnish

5 Add the chicken broth and salt, bring to a boil over medium-high heat, then stir in the rice and return to a boil, reduce the heat to medium, and simmer vigorously, stirring once in a while, until the rice is cooked and the soup thickens, about 20 minutes.

6 While the rice is cooking, whisk the eggs and lemon juice in a medium bowl until blended. Scoop 2 cups of the hot soup from the Dutch oven and, very slowly at first and whisking constantly, add it to the lemon-egg mixture (this prevents the eggs from scrambling), until the mixture is warmed and all 2 cups of soup are incorporated. Pour the mixture into the Dutch oven, stirring as you do, then add the chicken and pan juices to the pot and cook, stirring, for 2 minutes to warm through. Remove from the heat and add the oregano, season to taste with additional salt, and divide among bowls. Garnish with dill and some ground pepper.

hot & sour egg-"flick" soup

SERVES 6 TO 8
ACTIVE TIME: 25 MINUTES
TOTAL TIME: 1 HOUR 15 MINUTES
(INCLUDING MINIMUM MARINATING TIME)

I'm trying to write each *Cravings* book as a look into the current time. Book one was *very* much my life years ago: before kids, there were jokes about modeling; I remember being VERY pregnant with Luna right after its release, growing bigger with every book signing. The second book was written through terrible postpartum depression. And we are writing this one in the middle of a pandemic quarantine! I mean, I hope it isn't the middle. Ideally, it's closer to the end, since as I write this, we have been wearing masks for nine months now.

So, this soup. OOOOOO baby, this soup!! Thick, tart, perfectly reminiscent of the times we could go to Chinese restaurants. This is *exactly* that go-to hot-and-sour soup you get at your favorite little Chinese spot. The one that is ALWAYS there for you, the one that never changes, the one that you can always, always depend on.

There is one crucial element you need to make this look exactly like it does in that tall, clear takeout tub: strands of beaten egg that gently cook in the hot soup, floating like little lightning strikes. There are many ways to do it (check YouTube for videos galore!), but I like to use my (freshly washed and dried) fingers. While the soup is hot in the pot, I beat the eggs in a small bowl and dip my fingers into the egg, then flick the egg all over the top of the soup until it's all gone. Oh, you'll be soooo proud of this, I swear. It really is just the little things in life.

2 (8-ounce) skinless, boneless chicken breasts

¼ cup soy sauce, plus more as desired

3 tablespoons vegetable oil

3 garlic cloves, minced

6 ounces shiitake mushrooms, stems discarded, caps sliced ¼ inch thick (about 3 cups)

1 (8-ounce) can sliced bamboo shoots, drained

1 (15-ounce) can baby corn, drained and sliced crosswise into ¼-inch rounds (about 1⅓ cups)

8 cups low-sodium chicken broth

3 tablespoons unseasoned rice wine vinegar

2 teaspoons sweet chili sauce

2 teaspoons chili-garlic sauce

1½ teaspoons grated fresh ginger (from a 1-inch piece)

⅓ cup cornstarch

½ cup bean sprouts

3 scallions (green and white parts), thinly sliced

2 eggs

1 teaspoon toasted sesame oil

¼ teaspoon ground white pepper

1 In a large zippered plastic bag, combine the chicken, 2 tablespoons of the soy sauce, 1 tablespoon of the oil, and 1½ teaspoons of the minced garlic. Smoosh around, seal, and let sit on the counter for at least 30 minutes and up to 1 hour.

2 Heat another tablespoon of the oil in a large (at least 4-quart) Dutch oven over medium-high heat. Take the chicken from the bag, letting the excess marinade drip off, and sear the breasts until golden, 2 to 3 minutes per side. Transfer to a plate, leaving any juices in the pot.

3 Add the remaining tablespoon oil to the Dutch oven over medium-high heat, then add the mushrooms, bamboo shoots, corn, and remaining 1½ teaspoons garlic, along with ¼ cup of the broth, stirring occasionally and scraping the bottom to release any brown bits stuck on the bottom of the pot into the vegetables, and cook, stirring often, until mushrooms are just starting to soften, 3 minutes. Stir in the vinegar, remaining 2 tablespoons soy sauce, sweet chili sauce, chili-garlic sauce, and ginger.

4 Whisk the cornstarch with 1 cup of the broth in a small bowl until the mixture is smooth and has no clumps. Add it to the soup along with the remaining 6¾ cups broth, return the chicken breasts and any juices to the soup, bring the soup to a boil over high heat, reduce the heat to medium-low, and simmer, uncovered, stirring occasionally, until the soup thickens and the chicken is just cooked through, 7 to 8 minutes.

5 Remove the chicken from the soup and let cool for about 10 minutes. Meanwhile, continue simmering the soup uncovered, stirring occasionally. Shred the chicken into bite-sized pieces and return it to the soup. Season the soup to taste with additional soy sauce. Add the bean sprouts and scallions and return the soup to a boil over medium heat.

6 Whisk the eggs in a medium bowl with the sesame oil and white pepper, then use your fingers to flick the eggs into the soup; strands will form almost immediately. Gently stir the soup and then divide among bowls.

#potatoleeksoup

SERVES 6
ACTIVE TIME: 25 MINUTES
TOTAL TIME: 50 MINUTES

Soup alone is an incredible life invention, one with so many different possibilities, but soup that is able to form a hug around your entire body and bring you immeasurable comfort is . . . pretty special. This is that.

We had two ways to go with this soup—traditional and creamy, or the way we went: absolutely decadent, buttery, deeply flavorful, with bombs of soft potato pillows. I believe we chose right! And the hashtag-shaped dippers? (I know what you're thinking: "Chrissy, I have to make the soup AND stuff to go with it?") They represent the lattice-crust pattern of your favorite childhood pie. I originally had the idea of making this soup in a pie dish as an actual savory soup/pie hybrid thing (not all ideas work out, lol), but then I went with using these as a wonderful little dipper of sorts. You could *not* make this buttery little addition, sure, but you also could . . . and be way happier.

Soup

2¼ pounds waxy yellow potatoes, such as Yukon Gold

3 tablespoons unsalted butter

3 leeks (about 1½ pounds), cleaned and chopped (see Note, page 114)

2 teaspoons kosher salt, plus more for seasoning

5 garlic cloves, chopped

4½ cups low-sodium chicken broth, plus ½ cup more if necessary

1 cup (4 ounces) shredded cheddar cheese, plus more for garnish

1 cup heavy cream

Sliced fresh chives, for garnish

Hashtags

1 standard store-bought refrigerated pie crust, such as Pillsbury

1 egg, lightly beaten

Kosher salt

RECIPE CONTINUES

1 MAKE THE SOUP: Peel and cut the potatoes into 1½-inch chunks.

2 In a 4- or 5-quart saucepan, heat the butter over medium heat. Add the leeks and ½ teaspoon of the salt and cook, stirring occasionally, until the leeks soften and some are slightly golden, 8 minutes. Add the garlic and cook, stirring, until slightly softened, 3 minutes. Add the potatoes, the broth, and the remaining 1½ teaspoons salt. Bring to a boil, reduce the heat to a simmer, cover, and cook until the potatoes are tender, about 20 minutes.

3 Uncover the saucepan and use a slotted spoon to remove about ½ cup of the cooked potatoes, and reserve them. Working in batches if you have to, transfer the soup to a blender, leaving the lid a little ajar to release steam, and blend until smooth (you can also use an immersion/stick blender if you have one!). Return the soup to the pot, then mash the reserved potatoes until chunky and return them to the pot.

4 Add the 1 cup cheese and cream and stir them in. Cook over low heat until the cheese is melted and the soup thickens slightly, 5 minutes. Season to taste with more salt and thin with a little extra broth, if desired, and cover to keep warm.

5 MAKE THE HASHTAGS: Preheat the oven to 375°F. Lay the pie crust flat on a piece of parchment paper. Using a sharp paring knife or pizza cutter, cut some of the dough into ½-inch strips. (You will have a lot of dough; you can either make lots of hashtags or rewrap and refrigerate the remaining dough for another purpose!)

6 Cut the strips into 3½-inch lengths. Weave the strips into hashtag shapes, arrange them on a parchment-lined baking sheet, then brush them with egg and sprinkle with salt. Bake until golden and flaky, about 15 minutes. Hashtags can be stored in an airtight container for up to 2 days and can be rewarmed in a 325°F oven for 5 minutes.

7 Ladle the soup into bowls, sprinkle some cheddar on top of the soup, top each with a baked hashtag, and garnish with some chives.

Cleaning Leeks

Leave the fuzzy (root) end on the leeks, but trim the dark green ends so you are left with just a white/greenish piece of leek that is probably about 5 inches long. If the outside layer seems tough, peel it off and chuck it. Halve the leeks lengthwise, but don't cut all the way through the root end. Open the leeks a bit and put them in a large bowl of cold water. Let them sit for a minute, then open them a bit more to let any sand out. Drain and repeat. Drain again and dry, then trim off the roots and chop the leek.

chicken noodle matzo ball soup

SERVES 6 TO 8
ACTIVE TIME: 30 MINUTES
TOTAL TIME: 4 HOURS 15 MINUTES

There is a Jewish deli in L.A. called Nate 'n Al's, and it is pretty much an established fact that if you're feeling under the weather / feel a cold coming on / feeling the blues, what you need to do is Postmate, or actually get a loved one to *go* to Nate 'n Al's, wait in line, and get you the matzo ball soup.

But let me tell you a little something about me and matzo ball soup. I had it all of once in my life when I was living in NYC, and I was, like, "It's just not my thing." I assumed that the soup was *supposed* to taste like broth out of a box and the matzo ball was *supposed* to be a bland, chewy dough blob. This was just how it was and I didn't / don't love it, case closed. But that's not the case at all!

Adeena, who is Jewish, would be the obvious connection here. But it turns out that my paternal grandmother, Ruth Schaefer, was, too. It was a big day in our household when I put all the pieces together. My grandma was distanced by her family for not marrying a Jewish man, so my dad didn't grow up with a lot of his Jewish heritage, or eating a lot of traditional Jewish food.

Now, Adeena knows my exact tastes in food better than anybody else, which is an extremely intimate sort of relationship, and she told me she knew I would love this soup. I think she took it on as some sort of challenge, but she didn't have to work too hard. She adapted her late mom's recipe, which I am so grateful for. To share your household's family recipe and to have it published . . . sigh. The carrots, the onions, the broth. I tasted that broth and it was so fragging flavorful, the first thing Adeena said to me was, "No bouillon." That broth was so packed with flavor, it didn't need it.

Petey, our dog, ate half the chicken as it cooled on the counter, but the soup was still perfection. And I soon realized the matzo ball could be the most delicious, exciting part of the soup. (After all, it's a dumpling!) We made ours peppery and fluffy. Oh! And we added noodles, too. Adeena did say that it was the best version of a matzo ball soup that she had ever made, and that made me so happy—and makes this recipe incredibly special.

Matzo Balls

1 chicken bouillon cube

2 tablespoons boiling water

5 tablespoons vegetable oil

4 eggs

¼ teaspoon freshly ground black pepper

⅓ cup cold plain seltzer or club soda

1 cup matzo meal*

Soup

1 (4-pound) whole chicken, giblets removed

1 (10-ounce) skin-on, bone-in chicken breast

8 medium carrots, trimmed

3 large celery stalks, trimmed and halved crosswise

1 medium parsnip, trimmed and peeled

2 medium or 1 jumbo onion

4 garlic cloves

3 tablespoons kosher salt

½ (12-ounce) package fine (thin) egg noodles* (about 3¼ cups)

Chopped fresh dill, for garnish

*Matzo meal and fine egg noodles can be found in the tiny kosher/Jewish food section that exists in practically every supermarket.

RECIPE CONTINUES

1 MAKE THE MATZO BALL MIX: In a medium bowl, crumble the bouillon and dissolve it in the boiling water, whisking with a fork to make sure all the lumps are dissolved. Whisk in the oil first, and then the eggs and pepper, whisking vigorously until the color lightens, 30 seconds. Pour in the seltzer, followed by the matzo meal, and stir until the matzo meal is fully moistened and no clumps remain.

2 Press plastic wrap onto the surface of the mixture and chill while you make the soup, at least 3 hours and up to 24.

3 MAKE THE SOUP: While the matzo ball mix is chilling, place the whole chicken and chicken breast, carrots, celery, parsnip, onion, and garlic in a large (8-quart) pot, cover with water almost to the top (about 3½ quarts), add the salt, and bring to a boil over medium-high heat. Boil, skimming off and discarding any foam that rises to the surface, for 10 to 15 minutes.

4 Reduce the heat to low and simmer, uncovered, for 35 minutes more, then remove the chicken breast. Cool it until easy to handle, then remove and discard the skin and bones, and shred the meat. Cover and refrigerate until ready to use.

5 Continue to simmer the soup with the whole chicken until it deepens in color and the broth is chickeny and flavorful, about 3 hours.

6 During the last 45 minutes of cooking, fill a large, wide lidded pot halfway with water and season very generously with salt (it should taste like the sea). Bring it to a boil over medium-high heat.

7 Remove the matzo ball mix from the fridge. Fill a small bowl with water. Dip a tablespoon into the water, scoop out a heaping tablespoon of the batter, and use moistened hands to form a walnut-sized ball. Continue to make the balls; you should have about 16. Lower the balls into the boiling water, cover, reduce the heat to medium-low, and simmer until the matzo balls are fluffy, tender, and cooked through, 40 to 45 minutes.

8 Turn off the heat and leave the pot covered. (You can also make these a few hours early and leave them hanging out in the pot and liquid, then reheat over medium-low until just heated through, 10 to 15 minutes, until you're ready to use them.)

9 Bring a medium pot of generously salted water to a boil, then add the egg noodles and cook according to package directions; drain.

10 Using tongs, gently break the vegetables in the soup into pieces. To serve the soup, ladle some of the hot soup and vegetables into a bowl, then add 2 or 3 matzo balls, some noodles, and some shredded chicken. (You can also shred the dark meat from the whole chicken if you like dark-meat chicken better.*) Garnish with the dill.

*The meat from the chicken in the pot will have given up most of its flavor, but it would still be good chopped up for chicken salad or shredded and served in a flavorful sauce.

cozy classic
red lentil soup

SERVES 6 TO 8
ACTIVE TIME: 20 MINUTES
TOTAL TIME: 50 MINUTES

It's been a yearrrr. People use the term "life-changing" all the time, but when I tell you this warm, cozy soup upped my mood and got me through some of the roughest times, I am not kidding. Obviously, *Cravings* is about things that I want, make, and eat at the very moment that I want them. And there are many things that I have become obsessed with.

But nothing has hit me quite like this—this sneakily simple, classic, comforting soup. We sipped it out of giant mugs, warming our hands and dipping Sesame Parm Soupsticks (page 77), and the level of comfort and support I felt from this soup this year was off the charts. Batches were quadrupled (sextupled???), pot after pot was made, and when I tell you they were finished every time, they were finished every. single. time.

3 tablespoons olive oil

1 large yellow onion, cut into small dice

3 large carrots, cut into small dice

2 celery stalks, cut into small dice

4 garlic cloves, minced

7 cups low-sodium chicken broth*

1½ cups red lentils

1 tablespoon kosher salt, plus more for seasoning

¼ teaspoon freshly ground black pepper, plus more for seasoning

1 dried bay leaf

Chopped fresh parsley, for garnish

*If you only have 1 (4-cup) box of broth, you can supplement with water; just add a little bouillon or extra salt.

1 Heat the olive oil in a large (at least 4-quart) saucepan or small Dutch oven over medium heat. Add the onion and cook, stirring occasionally, until translucent but not browned, 7 to 8 minutes. Add the carrots, celery, and garlic, reduce the heat to medium-low, and cook, stirring occasionally, until the vegetables begin to soften, 5 to 7 minutes. Add the chicken broth, lentils, 1 tablespoon salt, ¼ teaspoon pepper, and the bay leaf, and stir.

2 Bring it all to a boil over medium-high heat, reduce the heat to medium-low to maintain a simmer, cover partially, and cook, stirring every 5 minutes or so, until the lentils are fully tender, break up, and the soup thickens and unifies, 25 to 30 minutes. Remove the bay leaf and season with more salt and pepper to taste. Garnish with the parsley.

spicy sausage pasta fagioli

SERVES 8 TO 10
ACTIVE TIME: 20 MINUTES
TOTAL TIME: 45 MINUTES

Within moments of eating this spicy pasta fagioli, we quickly realized it was going to become our new favorite soup (okay, co-favorite with the lentil soup, and the avgolemono, and, and, and . . .).

In creating this comforting, beautiful soup, we wanted to make sure every single bite has everything you need. There are beans. There are noodles. There is broth. There is sausage. It's hearty without making you feel weighed down, and for some reason you don't get tired of it.

Like most soup recipes, you can double or triple this recipe, portion it, and freeze it. All good ideas, since I don't ever see this as something you wouldn't want to have on hand. I mean, here in L.A., once the temperature dips below 65 degrees, everyone is bundled up like it's the North Pole; earmuffs and extra layers are employed, and our supreme wimpiness is revealed, so it's good to have this in the freezer at all times. (While we're on the subject, in New York City, the second it hits 55 degrees, Central Park is overflowing with people in swimsuit tops. What's up with that??)

2 tablespoons olive oil

1 pound hot Italian sausage, removed from casings if necessary

1 large yellow onion, diced

½ teaspoon dried rosemary

½ teaspoon dried thyme

3 medium carrots, diced

3 celery stalks, thinly sliced into half-moons

5 garlic cloves, thinly sliced

2 tablespoons tomato paste

4 cups low-sodium chicken broth

2 (15-ounce) cans cannellini or Great Northern beans, NOT drained or rinsed

1 (15-ounce) can fire-roasted (or regular) diced tomatoes

1 teaspoon kosher salt, plus more for seasoning

1¼ cups ditalini (or small elbow) pasta

1 cup (2 ounces) finely grated Parmigiano-Reggiano, plus more for garnish

4 cups baby spinach leaves

Freshly ground black pepper

1 Heat the olive oil in a large (at least 5-quart) deep pot or Dutch oven over medium-high heat. Add the sausage and cook, breaking up with a wooden spoon, until no longer pink, 5 to 6 minutes. Transfer the meat to a bowl with a slotted spoon, leaving any fat and juices in the pot.

2 Reduce the heat to medium and add the onion, rosemary, and thyme, and cook, stirring, until the onion begins to soften and turn slightly translucent, 5 to 6 minutes. Add the carrots, celery, and garlic and cook, stirring, until the vegetables begin to soften, 5 minutes. Add the tomato paste and cook, stirring, until absorbed into the vegetables, 2 minutes.

3 Return the sausage to the pot, then add the broth, beans with their liquid, tomatoes, and 1 teaspoon salt. Bring to a boil, then add the pasta and cook until it is tender and begins to release its starch, 10 to 12 minutes.

4 Stir in the 1 cup cheese and the spinach, which will wilt in about 30 seconds. Season to taste with more salt and pepper, divide the soup among bowls, and garnish with more cheese. As the soup sits, starch released from the pasta and beans turns the soup thick and stewy. If you love this (I do), keep serving it as is, but feel free to thin the soup out with a little water.

suppe

salmon quinoa salad

with carrot-ginger-miso dressing

SERVES 4
ACTIVE TIME: 15 MINUTES
TOTAL TIME: 50 MINUTES

I have told you before about the month-long period in my life, a few months after we had Luna, when we went on a trip to Bali to a wellness resort to restore my brain during a bout of postpartum depression. The food was such a highlight: super clean and healthy, but at the same time satisfying and flavorful. We did a few cooking classes there to understand the basics and make our favorites, and it was quickly apparent that dishes that SEEMED super easy were actually very complex. Things would be toasted or dehydrated for days before use or spices would be used that I've never heard of and definitely don't remember.

Something very special I had was a quinoa salad with corn and arugula. It had herbs and spices and juice from fruits I'd never before seen. We would have them top the dish with the rarest piece of salmon—one of the only foods I believe can be enjoyed both well-done AND rare-rare.

So sometimes I try to re-create that experience at home, but without all those ingredients I don't know the names of, and this comes out. We cook the salmon but still leave it tender, and I came up with a totally different but totally ENHANCED dressing. When we order Japanese takeout, I can never decide between carrot-ginger dressing and miso dressing. I want it all, so behold, we can have it ALL! I just ask that you not limit the use of this dressing to this recipe. It's too good.

Dressing

1 medium carrot, diced

½ cup neutral-flavored oil, such as safflower, canola, or vegetable

3 tablespoons unseasoned rice vinegar

3 tablespoons light brown sugar

2 tablespoons light miso paste

1 tablespoon minced fresh ginger (from a 1-inch piece)

1 large garlic clove

2 teaspoons toasted sesame oil

Salmon & Quinoa

1 cup quinoa

Kosher salt and freshly ground black pepper

4 (6-ounce) center-cut salmon fillets

2½ tablespoons olive oil

1 teaspoon ground cumin

1 (14-ounce) can sweet corn kernels, drained

1 cup drained and rinsed canned black beans

3 cups baby arugula leaves

¼ cup thinly sliced red onion

1 MAKE THE DRESSING: Combine all the dressing ingredients in a blender and blend until smooth-ish (but you still see some semblance of carrot), 20 to 30 seconds. Transfer to a container and chill until ready to use. (Makes 1 generous cup.)

2 PREPARE THE QUINOA AND SALMON: Arrange a rack in the upper third of the oven. Preheat the oven to 325°F.

3 Rinse the quinoa with cold water until the water runs clear. Place it in a small saucepan and cover it with generously salted water by 1 inch. Bring to a boil, reduce the heat to medium, then cover, leaving a small crack open, and cook, opening the pot and stirring every 5 minutes, until all the water has evaporated and the quinoa is fluffy and separated, 20 minutes (stir more toward the end to prevent the quinoa from sticking and burning). Turn the quinoa out onto a rimmed baking sheet and spread it out to cool. (This helps any remaining water evaporate and keeps the quinoa from being waterlogged and soggy.)

4 Meanwhile, rub the salmon with about 1½ tablespoons of the olive oil, then sprinkle all over with the cumin and season generously with salt and pepper. Place the salmon fillets on a baking sheet and roast in the oven until just cooked through but still juicy and tender, about 17 minutes. Remove from oven and cover to keep warm.

5 Change the oven setting to broil and allow briefly to preheat. Arrange the corn on a foil-lined baking sheet. Toss with the remaining 1 tablespoon oil, then broil until the kernels char slightly, 5 minutes.

6 Gently toss together the quinoa, corn, black beans, arugula, and red onion slices. Divide among 4 plates, then top each plate with a salmon fillet and drizzle with the dressing.

shawarma-spiced skirt steak salad

SERVES 4
ACTIVE TIME: 35 MINUTES
TOTAL TIME: 2 HOURS 35 MINUTES
(INCLUDING MINIMUM MARINATING TIME)

Steak salad can be a little boring, so we added cumin and turmeric and that meat-on-a-spit goodness you find all over the Middle East (and all over the world, really, since shawarma is superpopular).

Eating this is fun because you can dig around and construct the perfect bite: a piece of tomato, the spice-infused meat, the charred onion, a crunchy pita chip, some lemony dressing, and a bit of feta. I admit that I was not the biggest feta fan before we added it here, but I think learning to love something qualifies as personal growth.

Steak & Onions

⅓ cup olive oil

6 garlic cloves, smashed

1 teaspoon finely grated lemon zest

1¼ teaspoons ground turmeric

1 teaspoon ground coriander

1 teaspoon ground cumin

½ teaspoon cayenne pepper

1 teaspoon kosher salt, plus more for seasoning

½ teaspoon freshly ground black pepper, plus more for seasoning

½ teaspoon onion powder

1½ pounds boneless skirt steak or flap steak

1 medium yellow onion, sliced into half-moons

Dressing & Salad

½ cup olive oil

3 tablespoons fresh lemon juice

1 teaspoon Dijon mustard

¼ teaspoon kosher salt, plus more for seasoning

1 (7- to 9-ounce) package chopped romaine lettuce

1 cup cherry tomatoes, halved

½ cup (2 ounces) crumbled feta cheese

½ small red onion, sliced into half-moons

½ cup crumbled pita chips, flavor of your choice (we like Stacy's)

Freshly ground black pepper

1 **PREPARE THE STEAK:** In a plastic bag, combine the olive oil, garlic, lemon zest, 1 teaspoon of the turmeric, the coriander, cumin, cayenne, 1 teaspoon salt, ½ teaspoon pepper, and onion powder. Add the steak and move it around in the bag. Let the meat sit on the counter for 2 hours, or in the fridge for up to 24 hours.

2 Heat a large grill pan, cast-iron skillet, or grill over high heat for 4 minutes. Remove the steak from the bag and cut into pieces that will fit in the pan without crowding. Sear the meat, without moving, until it is blackened in parts, about 3 minutes per side. Remove to a plate and cover to keep warm.

3 Lower the heat to medium, then add the onion and remaining ¼ teaspoon turmeric. Cook, stirring occasionally, until the onion is charred but still tender-crisp, 4 to 5 minutes. Season with salt and pepper and transfer to a plate.

4 **MAKE THE DRESSING AND SALAD:** In a jar, combine the olive oil, lemon juice, mustard, and salt, seal, and shake well.

5 Arrange the lettuce and tomatoes on a platter. Slice the steak into ½-inch strips and scatter it with the onions and lettuce. Crumble the feta on top, drizzle with the dressing, top with the pita chips, and season with salt and pepper.

crispy
chicken-caesar
wedge salad

SERVES 4
ACTIVE TIME: 40 MINUTES
TOTAL TIME: 40 MINUTES

I can't decide if I love or hate a meal that makes you work for it. I do know that I love the ballsiness of a restaurant saying, "Put it together your damn self!" and what I *also* know is that John HATES it. I'm the one shelling his crab, peeling his shrimp. I'm the one cooking his meat at the Korean BBQ. He barely likes putting his raw, thinly sliced steak into his pho. Basically, all this man wants to do is chew.

Anyhow, I *do* love a wedge salad, which is basically a big uncut slab of lettuce. I like to mix it up a bit: a thin fork shred one minute, maybe the next bite a large chunky triangle. I dunno! Who knows?! The chaos! What an adventure! I went with the crazy and mixed the DNAs of Caesar and Wedge, and this is the result. Once again, I've done all the work, John . . . enjoy!

1½ cups (3 ounces) finely grated Parmigiano-Reggiano cheese

¾ cup mayonnaise

¼ cup fresh lemon juice (from about 1 lemon)

2 garlic cloves, very finely minced

1½ teaspoons fish sauce

1 teaspoon freshly ground black pepper, plus more for seasoning

¼ teaspoon cayenne pepper

1¼ cups panko bread crumbs

¾ teaspoon kosher salt, plus more for seasoning

½ cup flour

4 (4- or 5-ounce) thin-cut chicken breasts (about 1 pound total)

4 slices bacon

1 medium head iceberg lettuce

Vegetable oil, for frying

1 cup cherry tomatoes, halved

½ cup (2 ounces) crumbled blue cheese

1 Preheat the oven to 400°F.

2 In a medium bowl, whisk together 1 cup of the parm with the mayo, lemon juice, garlic, fish sauce, 1 teaspoon pepper, and cayenne. Measure ½ cup of the dressing and place it in a separate bowl.

3 In a shallow bowl, combine the panko, remaining ½ cup parm, and ½ teaspoon salt.

4 In a zippered plastic bag, combine the flour and remaining ¼ teaspoon salt. Add the chicken to the bag and shake to coat well. Transfer the chicken from the bag to a plate, then brush each cutlet with 2 tablespoons of the dressing (1 tablespoon per side). Press both sides of each cutlet into the panko, applying pressure to make crumbs adhere. Place the cutlets on a plate and set aside.

5 Arrange the bacon on a small foil-lined baking sheet and bake until crisped and the fat is rendered, 13 to 14 minutes. Transfer the bacon to a paper towel–lined plate to drain and cool, then crumble it.

6 Cut the iceberg head in half, then cut out and discard the core. Cut each half in half again to form 4 wedges.

7 Add enough vegetable oil to a 10-inch skillet to create a ¼-inch layer and heat it over medium heat until a panko crumb sizzles upon contact. Fry the cutlets until golden, 3 to 4 minutes per side. Drain on paper towels, then slice into strips.

8 Arrange 1 lettuce wedge on a dinner plate, then add a fourth of the cutlet slices, ¼ cup sliced tomatoes, one-fourth of the crumbled bacon (about 2 tablespoons), and 2 tablespoons blue cheese. Drizzle about 3 tablespoons dressing on the salad and season with more salt and lots of pepper.

grilled shrimp pasta salad
with creamy lemon dressing

SERVES 6
ACTIVE TIME: 20 MINUTES
TOTAL TIME: 30 MINUTES

I love a creamy pasta salad, but honestly, so many of them . . . suck. Too often, the dressing soaks into the pasta and disappears into flavor oblivion. I only want to deliver you something you would be excited to make!

And so I present this slippery, lemony shrimpy number that absolutely, positively knocks it out of the park. The dressing is blended avocado (yep), lemon, and olive oil, which beautifully coats the pasta and makes it . . . dare I say? . . . healthy, but rich and indulgent without weighing you down after you eat it. The charred shrimp feel special, but you could also swap in chunks of cooked salmon or tuna. This would make a great room-temp buffet dish or cold picnic item; it holds super well and maintains its flavor and, if you cook the 'ghetti al dente, its texture.

1½ pounds jumbo (16 to 20 per pound) shrimp, peeled and deveined

½ cup plus 1½ tablespoons olive oil

1½ teaspoons finely grated lemon zest

6 garlic cloves, 3 thinly sliced

1½ teaspoons kosher salt, plus more for seasoning

¼ teaspoon freshly ground black pepper, plus more for seasoning

¼ teaspoon cayenne pepper

1 (1-pound) package spaghetti

⅔ cup fresh lemon juice (from about 2 large lemons)

½ medium avocado

¾ pound (4 medium) Persian cucumbers, peeled and cut into thin strips

3 cups (1 pound) multicolored cherry tomatoes, halved

1 small jalapeño pepper, very thinly sliced (seeded, if desired)

2 ounces Parmigiano-Reggiano cheese, finely grated (1 cup), plus more for garnish

½ cup shredded fresh basil, plus more for garnish

---

1 Toss the shrimp, 1½ tablespoons of the olive oil, the lemon zest, 3 sliced garlic cloves, ½ teaspoon salt, ¼ teaspoon pepper, and the cayenne in a bowl to marinate while you make the pasta.

2 Meanwhile, bring a large pot of heavily salted water to a boil. Cook the spaghetti according to package directions, until al dente. Rinse well under cold water, then drain thoroughly.

3 While the pasta is cooking, make the dressing by combining the lemon juice, remaining ½ cup olive oil, the avocado, 3 remaining garlic cloves, and 1 teaspoon salt in a blender and blend until smooth and creamy, 30 seconds.

4 Toss the pasta, dressing, cucumbers, tomatoes, and jalapeño in a large bowl until everything is well coated.

5 Heat a large cast-iron skillet over high heat. Scrape the garlic off the marinated shrimp and cook the shrimp, not moving them, until lightly browned and bright pink, 1 to 1½ minutes per side. Season to taste with salt and pepper.

6 Toss the parm and basil into the pasta, season to taste with salt and pepper, then transfer the salad to a serving platter and top with the shrimp. Garnish with more cheese and basil.

corned (& ground) beef stuffed cab—bage rolls

MAKES 12 ROLLS, SERVING 6
ACTIVE TIME: 40 MINUTES
TOTAL TIME: 2 HOURS 30 MINUTES

I grew the eff UP on corned beef and cabbage. If you've ever seen a pic of Pops Teigen, you'll immediately see that I'm Irish-adjacent enough to have had this dish as least 300 times in my life. Usually it's a wedge of boiled cabbage (exciting!!) plated alongside 2 or 3 slices of juicy, peppery corned beef. We bought the corned beef, always, from Costco—a big hunk of beef, sealed in plastic. Some people are nostalgic for family heirlooms; I am nostalgic for Costco corned beef in a bag.

This is basically corned beef and cabbage in cabbage-roll form—done to feed the entire family for a couple of wonderful nights. Usually cabbage rolls are made with much more vinegar, but I wanted mine to lean into the sweeter side, so I tilted it toward brown sugar. If you don't have one or the other of the canned tomatoes products, feel free to double up on one of them, but do not skimp on the garlic, and welcome this new family favorite into your life!

1 large head green cabbage

3 tablespoons vegetable oil

1 jumbo yellow onion, diced

2 tablespoons minced garlic

1 (28-ounce) can crushed tomatoes, with juice

1 (28-ounce) can tomato sauce

½ cup light brown sugar

2 tablespoons white vinegar, or more to taste

2 teaspoons kosher salt, plus more for seasoning

1 teaspoon red pepper flakes

1½ pounds ground beef

½ pound cooked corned beef, finely chopped

1 cup fresh bread crumbs

½ cup uncooked white rice

2 eggs, lightly beaten

¼ cup finely chopped fresh parsley

1 tablespoon deli, spicy brown, or grainy Dijon mustard

½ teaspoon freshly ground black pepper, plus more for seasoning

RECIPE CONTINUES

1　Fill a very large pot two-thirds of the way with lightly salted water and bring to a boil. While the water is coming to a boil, cut the core out of the cabbage, cutting about ½ inch around the core at the bottom and 2 inches deep so you can pull out the core, sort of like pulling a plug out of a drain.

2　When the pot of water has come to a boil, gently lower the cabbage into the pot and make sure the cut side is submerged in the water. As the leaves peel off, let them sit in the water for 1 extra minute to soften, then transfer them to a colander to drain and cool. (You need 12 leaves, but 13 never hurt in case one rips and you need to start over.)

3　While the cabbage is cooking, heat the vegetable oil in a large (at least 4-quart) saucepan over medium heat. Add the onion and cook, stirring often, until lightly golden, 9 to 10 minutes. Add the garlic and cook, stirring, 1 minute.

4　Transfer half the onion-garlic mixture to a large bowl to cool.

5　Add the crushed tomatoes, tomato sauce, brown sugar, vinegar, 1 teaspoon of the salt, and ½ teaspoon of the red pepper flakes to the saucepan. Bring to a boil, reduce the heat to low, and simmer until the sauce slightly thickens, 10 to 15 minutes.

6　To the bowl with the cooled onion-garlic mixture add the ground beef, corned beef, bread crumbs, rice, eggs, parsley, mustard, remaining 1 teaspoon salt, ½ teaspoon pepper, and remaining ½ teaspoon red pepper flakes. Combine the mixture with your hands until well blended.

7　Preheat the oven to 350°F. Spoon a generous one-third of the tomato sauce into the bottom of a 9 × 13-inch glass baking dish.

8　Arrange a softened cabbage leaf on a clean work surface and place about ⅓ cup meat filling centered on the bottom third of the cabbage leaf. Bring the bottom over to cover the filling, then fold in the sides and roll over to seal (just like making a burrito!). Place the cabbage roll in the baking dish, then repeat with the remaining cabbage leaves and filling (you should have 12 rolls).

9　Pour the rest of the sauce over the cabbage, then use a knife to move them around a little so the sauce gets between the rolls. Cover well with foil and bake until the cabbage is very tender and all the flavors have melded, 1½ hours. Remove the foil and continue to bake until the sauce is slightly thickened, an additional 10 minutes.

10　Transfer the rolls to plates and spoon the sauce over to serve.

beef stroganoff

with buttered salt & pepper noodles

SERVES 6
ACTIVE TIME: 35 MINUTES
TOTAL TIME: 45 MINUTES

There have been countless cookbooks devoted to moms sneaking healthy ingredients into their kids' food, but I could probably fill the pages of an entire volume with recipes that swap in Asian condiments where other ones were originally called for. Exhibit A: this stroganoff. Yes, you've seen and probably made sour-creamy beef stroganoff before, but I guarantee you one made with soy sauce and fish sauce has never graced the pages of Betty Crocker.

Fish sauce stands in for Worcestershire perfectly (after all, they both contain anchovies!), but it adds way more umami punch. And soy sauce . . . ever since I used it to jack up my French onion soup in my last book, it's become a favorite go-to for savory success. What comes out is the thinly sliced steak, onions, 'shrooms, and sour cream you know and love, but with way more depth of flavor, clinging to the buttery, peppery wide egg noodles.

1 pound cremini or button mushrooms

2½ cups low-sodium beef broth

¼ cup flour

1½ teaspoons fish sauce, plus more for seasoning

1¼ pounds trimmed boneless ribeye steak, thinly sliced

2 tablespoons low-sodium soy sauce

3 garlic cloves, minced

1 teaspoon freshly ground black pepper

3 tablespoons unsalted butter

3 tablespoons vegetable oil

2 medium yellow onions, thinly sliced

½ cup sour cream

Kosher salt

1 (1-pound) package wide egg noodles

¼ cup minced fresh chives

RECIPE CONTINUES

1 Bring a large pot of generously salted water to a boil, reduce the heat to low, and cover until ready to use.

2 Trim the ends of the stems off the mushrooms if they look brown. Cut the mushrooms into quarters (or halves, if they're small).

3 Reserve ¼ cup of the broth. Whisk the remaining 2¼ cups broth with the flour and 1½ teaspoons fish sauce in a medium bowl until the flour is dissolved.

4 Toss the meat with 1 tablespoon of the soy sauce, the garlic, and ½ teaspoon pepper. Heat 1 tablespoon of the butter and 2 tablespoons of the oil in a large skillet over high heat until the butter foams. Add the meat in as close to a single layer as possible and cook without stirring, until the underside is a little seared, 2 to 3 minutes. Stir and cook until the meat is no longer pink, another 1 to 2 minutes. Transfer the meat to a medium bowl, leaving as much of the juice in the pan as possible. Toss the meat with the remaining tablespoon soy sauce.

5 Lower the heat to medium-high and add the remaining 1 tablespoon oil to the skillet, then add the onions and cook, stirring, until softened and just golden, 6 to 7 minutes. Add the mushrooms along with the reserved ¼ cup broth and cook, stirring occasionally, until the mushrooms cook off their liquid and turn slightly golden, another 5 to 6 minutes.

6 Re-stir the broth-flour mixture and add it to the skillet. Bring to a boil, reduce the heat to medium, and simmer until the mixture thickens, 3 to 4 minutes. Stir in the meat and any accumulated juices, along with the sour cream, then simmer an additional 3 minutes. Season to taste with salt and more fish sauce. Turn off the heat and cover to keep warm.

7 Return the pot of water to a boil and cook the egg noodles according to package directions. (If you are a kitchen timing master, you can do this while you're still cooking the sauce.) Drain the noodles, then toss in a large bowl with the remaining 2 tablespoons butter, ½ teaspoon pepper, and the chives. Season to taste with salt and serve with the stroganoff.

yai's thai sloppy joes

SERVES 4
ACTIVE TIME: 20 MINUTES
TOTAL TIME: 25 MINUTES

I forget: Did we all f*cking LOVE sloppy joe day in school or did we hate it?? I *believe* I loved it, but I also have images in my head of those commercials in which angry lunch ladies used their giant spoons to aggressively bang it onto your plastic tray. Which by the way, is so unfair. Lunch ladies are always portrayed so horribly! Who created this fantasy in the first place? They feed your kids! Be nice to them!

Anyhow, I would *live* for sloppy joe day now, because our super-easy Thai pita version was the absolute BEST thing to shoot in this entire book. No, pitas are not the traditional vehicle for sloppy joes, and coconut milk and fish sauce weren't in my cafeteria either, but who cares? We ate about three of these each . . . on *both* photo shoots. Because, full disclosure: Mom has *her* recipe for these in her book, and now I have stolen the recipe and made it my own because I wanted to make sure that you had it. You deserve this recipe once, twice, three times a shady (daughter). Consider these my sloppy seconds.

2 tablespoons vegetable oil

½ medium yellow onion, finely minced

6 garlic cloves, minced

1 pound ground beef

¼ cup tomato paste

¼ teaspoon ground white pepper

¼ teaspoon cayenne pepper

1 cup red or yellow cherry tomatoes, quartered

½ cup diced red bell pepper

2 tablespoons full-fat coconut milk

1 tablespoon blond miso paste

1 tablespoon fish sauce, plus more for seasoning

1 tablespoon dark brown sugar

4 pocket pitas

12 medium butter lettuce leaves

1 large vine-ripened tomato, cut into thin rounds

1 In a large skillet, heat the oil over medium heat. Add the onion and cook, stirring, until it begins to soften, 5 to 6 minutes. Add the garlic and cook, stirring, 1 more minute.

2 Add the beef and cook, stirring and breaking up with a wooden spoon, until just barely no longer pink, about 4 minutes. Add the tomato paste, white pepper, and cayenne and cook, stirring, until caramelized, 2 to 3 minutes. Add the cherry tomatoes and bell pepper and cook, stirring, until the tomatoes melt a bit, 2 to 3 minutes. Add the coconut milk, miso paste, fish sauce, and brown sugar and cook, stirring, until a slightly thick sauce forms, 2 to 3 minutes. Season with a drop more fish sauce, if you feel like it. Remove the skillet from the heat.

3 Warm the pitas over a gas flame or by wrapping them in a slightly damp cloth and microwaving for 30 seconds. Stuff each pita with 2 lettuce leaves, a tomato slice, and one-fourth of the meat mixture.

meatloaf wellington

SERVES 8
ACTIVE TIME: 40 MINUTES
TOTAL TIME: 2 HOURS

A traditional beef Wellington is like the ultimate in fancy. It's a whole beef tenderloin— a.k.a. the entire roast that filet mignon comes from—that's been stuffed with mushrooms and wrapped in crispy puff pastry (which is in itself a massive test of pastry chef skill). If I say so myself, every Christmas, I make a pretty incredible beef Wellington. And I do it just by riffing off a few recipes I see online, so the secrets to success are OUT THERE. But I wanted to share a Wellington recipe with you. I needed to give you something different. And voilà, this recipe was born.

And this one is so good it will make you NEVER WANT TO MAKE TRADITIONAL BEEF WELLINGTON. It's a true miracle of science— how easily this recipe comes together. Instead of using a giant beef tenderloin, which is $$$$ and easy to overcook, we use the most beautiful meatloaf mix. And instead of borrrrrring breadcrumbs, we use crunched-up Stove Top stuffing because why does no one ever do this?!?!?!!!?!! The meat is juicy, the puff pastry is crispy (and from a box), and it feeds loads of your friends and/or family. It is THE perfect Sunday dinner, or honestly for any day of the week.

1 (17.3-ounce) package Pillsbury puff pastry sheets (2 sheets), defrosted according to package instructions

Flour, for rolling pastry (optional)

2 tablespoons olive oil

1 medium onion, finely diced

1 tablespoon minced garlic

1 (8-ounce) package fresh cremini or button mushrooms, stems discarded, very finely chopped (about 1½ cups)

2 teaspoons kosher salt

½ teaspoon freshly ground black pepper

1 (6-ounce) package chicken-flavored Stove Top stuffing mix

3 eggs

1½ pounds (at least 80/20) ground beef

1 cup (2 ounces) finely grated Parmigiano-Reggiano cheese

¼ teaspoon cayenne pepper

6 ounces (about 12 slices) thinly sliced prosciutto

RECIPE CONTINUES

1 Open up the puff pastry package and roll out (on a lightly floured surface, if needed) one sheet to about 12 inches square. Roll the other one to 10 inches square, then cut a 9 × 5-inch piece out of it. Place both pieces on a tray lined with parchment paper. Refrigerate the pastry sheets and scraps (to make cool shapes for the top!) while preparing the loaf.

2 In a large skillet, over medium heat, warm the olive oil. Add the onion and cook, stirring, until lightly golden, 9 to 10 minutes. Add the garlic and cook, stirring, 1 minute. Add the mushrooms, ½ teaspoon salt, and ¼ teaspoon pepper. Raise the heat to medium-high and cook, stirring often, until the mushrooms release their water and the skillet is dry, 6 to 7 minutes. Cool for 15 minutes.

3 Preheat the oven to 400°F.

4 Place the stuffing mix in a blender or processor and process until fine crumbs form (about 15 seconds); or place in a zippered plastic bag, seal, and crush into fine crumbs (you should have a generous ½ cup crumbs).

5 In a large bowl, beat 2 of the eggs, then stir in the stuffing crumbs to moisten. Add the mushroom mixture, ground beef, parm, remaining 1½ teaspoons salt and ¼ teaspoon pepper, and the cayenne. Gently mix with your hands until everything is incorporated, trying not to overmix.

6 Line a rimmed baking sheet with parchment paper. Place the 9 x 5-inch pastry piece on the parchment in the center of the baking sheet. Lay 6 slightly overlapping strips of prosciutto crosswise on the pastry, with the ends of the prosciutto overhanging the pastry on both sides.

7 Shape the meat mixture into a 9 × 5-inch loaf and center it on the prosciutto. Bring the ends of the prosciutto up the sides of the meatloaf, then arrange the remaining 6 slices of prosciutto lengthwise over the top of the meatloaf so the sides and top of the loaf are now encased in prosciutto.

8 Place the 12-inch square of pastry on top of the loaf on the diagonal, so that the pointed tips of the square extend beyond the ends of the loaf. (This gives you more length to cover the loaf.) Moisten the edges of the pastry all over with water, then tuck the ends of the top pastry down and under the loaf, sealing to the bottom pastry edge as much as possible. Beat the remaining egg, and brush the Wellington lightly with some of the egg.

9 Cut three 1-inch slits along the top of the Wellington, then use the pastry scraps to cut cool shapes and attach them to the top, brushing them with a bit of the beaten egg. Place the loaf in the oven and bake until the crust begins to turn deep golden, 25 to 30 minutes.

10 Reduce the heat to 375°F and bake until the meat inside reaches about 155°F on an instant-read meat thermometer, another 25 to 30 minutes, tenting with foil to prevent excess browning, if needed. Remove from the oven, let rest for 10 minutes to help the juices settle in the loaf, then use a serrated knife to cut into 1-inch pieces.

beer-braised short rib burritos

MAKES 6 BURRITOS
ACTIVE TIME: 40 MINUTES
TOTAL TIME: 4 HOURS (PLUS OPTIONAL OVERNIGHT CHILLING)

Los Angeles is home to *truly* some of the best burrito places in the world. This is a huge statement to make, I know, but I feel confident in saying it because of places like Escuela Taqueria, home of the creamy bean-filled tortilla of greatness that inspired this burrito. The thick sauciness of the burrito filling is what separates this from every other—it's almost like you could get it out into a bowl and eat it with a spoon (which, why not?).

Our take on this L.A. staple uses beef short rib because it's almost guaranteed to stay juicy. We add black beans and canned green chiles (soo easy), and it contains so much flavor you might just slap your Yai. To further customize it, we topped the tortilla with cheese and warmed it to the melting point before wrapping and, my God, I can't express enough how good of an idea this was.

It's kind of not worth braising short ribs unless you do a bunch of meat, so if you don't feel like making all six burritos at once, this filling will last in the fridge for up to 5 days, and you can make burritos whenever the urge strikes. Or, you could warm some filling and serve over rice with salsa and avocados.

We also re-created our take on Escuela's simple, smoky, spicy salsa, and couldn't be happier with the results. I LOVE YOU, L.A.

3 pounds bone-in beef short ribs, cut English-style* into 3-inch pieces

2 teaspoons kosher salt, plus more for seasoning

½ teaspoon freshly ground black pepper, plus more for seasoning

1 large onion, diced

8 garlic cloves

1 teaspoon seeded and chopped jalapeño pepper

1½ cups lager-style beer, such as Corona, Negro Modelo, or Heineken

1¼ cups low-sodium beef broth

2 (15-ounce) cans black beans, drained

1 (7-ounce) can diced green chiles, drained

½ cup chopped fresh cilantro

6 burrito-sized (10-inch) soft wheat tortillas

1½ cups (6 ounces) shredded extra-sharp cheddar cheese

Spicy Homemade Salsa (recipe follows)

*"English style" means the short ribs are cut so that they look like something from the *Flintstones*— a big bone with a hunk of meat wrapped around it.

RECIPE CONTINUES

1 Pat the ribs dry, then season them generously on both sides with salt and pepper. Heat a dry (no oil) large heavy Dutch oven over medium-high heat. Working in batches if you have to, add the short ribs and sear until deeply browned on all sides, 4 minutes per side.

2 Remove the short ribs to a plate, then add the onion, garlic, and jalapeño to the fat in the Dutch oven, reduce the heat to medium-low, and cook, stirring, until the onion is tender and translucent, about 10 minutes.

3 Add the ribs back to the pot along with the beer, beef broth, 2 teaspoons salt, and ½ teaspoon pepper. Raise the heat to high to bring to a boil, reduce the heat to a low simmer, cover, and cook until the ribs are fork-tender and falling off the bone, 3 to 3½ hours. If you have time, cool the ribs and cooking liquid, then refrigerate them separately overnight to let the fat solidify; skim and remove the fat, then remove and discard the bones. Otherwise, do your best to skim the liquid fat off with a spoon. Or just eat it all if you don't care.

4 When ready to serve, warm the meat in the sauce over medium heat for about 15 minutes. If you have not already done so, gently pull the meat into smaller chunks and remove the bones.

5 Mash the beans in a medium bowl until some are fully mashed and some are partially whole. Add them to the short ribs along with the chiles and cilantro, then season to taste with more salt and pepper.

6 Heat a dry 10-inch nonstick skillet (make sure it has a lid) over medium heat for 2 to 3 minutes, then add a tortilla to the skillet and sprinkle ¼ cup of the cheese into the center of the tortilla. Cover and warm until the cheese is melted and the underside of the tortilla is crisp, 3 to 4 minutes.

7 Uncover the tortilla, transfer to a cutting board, then add about 1¼ cups of the meat filling along the bottom third of it, leaving about 4 inches on the bottom and 3 inches on the sides. Pull the bottom of the tortilla over the filling, then fold the sides into the center and roll the burrito away from you until closed. Wrap in parchment paper, then wrap in foil, and continue to make the remaining burritos. Slice through the centers of each with a serrated knife, and serve in the foil for the full burrito-shop effect.

SPICY HOMEMADE SALSA
MAKES 1½ CUPS
ACTIVE TIME: 5 MINUTES
TOTAL TIME: 20 MINUTES

1 pound firm, ripe tomatoes

1 medium jalapeño pepper

¼ cup finely diced onion

2 tablespoons chopped fresh cilantro

2 teaspoons fresh lime juice (from 1 small lime)

1 teaspoon kosher salt

½ teaspoon finely minced garlic

Heat a dry (no oil) medium cast-iron skillet over medium-high heat. Add the tomatoes and jalapeño and char, turning every minute or so, until the tomatoes are blackened in spots but not mushy and the jalapeño is softened and blackened, 10 minutes. Cool, remove and discard the cores from the tomatoes and the stem from the jalapeño, and blend in a food processor or blender until mostly smooth, 5 to 10 seconds. Transfer to a bowl and stir in the onion, cilantro, lime juice, salt, and garlic.

special-occasion prime rib roast

SERVES 8 TO 10

ACTIVE TIME: 35 MINUTES

TOTAL TIME: ABOUT 6 HOURS, MOSTLY JUST SITTING THERE

By now you all know how I feel about a Thanksgiving turkey. (If you don't, know that the feelings are NOT GOOD.) And though I put on a brave face about it, I was less than thrilled with the prospect of yet another year with a giant, dry bird as the centerpiece of my favorite meal of the year, especially last year, when joy on the table was absolutely necessary. And then, Then, THEN! This roast.

I had always approached a huge bone-in standing rib roast like I had approached bread: like a scaredy cat watching *Ratched* with one eye half open. There is just so much at stake (steak? hahaha) when you invest this much time and energy and money in a piece of meat, because prime rib is downright pricey. But THIS meat, guys! Slathered with herb butter and finished with a wine-and-mustard sauce, our poor turkey didn't stand a chance this year. And it's going to have to get used to second billing, because from now on prime rib IS the new Thanksgiving turkey in our house.

Read the whole recipe through and you'll realize that most of the prep time just involves waiting for the meat to come to room temp; then, after a hot sear, it cooks nice and slow until there's a beautiful crust and rosy, juicy meat that's as buttery, tender, and flavorful as anything you have ever tasted.

Roast

1 (8-pound) bone-in prime rib (standing rib roast); should have 3 or 4 ribs

1 tablespoon kosher salt, plus more for seasoning

1 stick (8 tablespoons) unsalted butter, at room temperature

¼ cup finely chopped garlic (from 10 to 12 cloves)

8 fresh thyme sprigs, plus 1½ teaspoons chopped leaves

8 fresh rosemary sprigs, plus 1½ teaspoons chopped leaves

2 teaspoons Dijon mustard

½ teaspoon freshly ground black pepper, plus more for seasoning

4 large shallots, halved crosswise

Sauce

1½ cups dry white wine

2 tablespoons Dijon mustard

1 tablespoon honey

1 tablespoon water

2 teaspoons cornstarch

RECIPE CONTINUES

1 **MOST IMPORTANT STEP:** Bring the meat to room temperature! Take it out of the fridge and let it rest uncovered on the counter for 2 hours; nothing is going to happen to you or your meat! This allows the meat to cook evenly and the inside and outside to be ready at the same rate so that it will achieve beautiful, uniform doneness.

2 **ROAST THE MEAT:** Preheat the oven to 475°F. Set a rack somewhere between the center and lower third of the oven. Place the meat, bone side down, in a roasting pan (preferably something 2 to 3 inches larger than the roast on all sides but not much more) and season all over with 2 teaspoons salt. Roast until the fat starts to crackle and char a bit, about 18 minutes.

3 Meanwhile, in a bowl, combine the butter, garlic, chopped thyme and rosemary, mustard, remaining 1 teaspoon salt, and ½ teaspoon pepper.

4 Reduce the oven to 325°F, remove the roast from the oven, and let cool for 10 minutes. Place the shallots, 5 of the thyme sprigs, and 5 of the rosemary sprigs in the pan. Spread the garlic-herb butter on the meat/fat side of the roast, return the roast to the oven, and cook until the internal temperature reaches 115°F on a meat thermometer (it will continue to rise as it rests), about 2 hours, basting the roast every 45 minutes or so with the fat from the pan. Remove the roast from the oven, loosely tent it with foil, and let it rest for 20 to 25 minutes.

5 **MAKE THE SAUCE:** Remove the shallots and herb sprigs from the pan and pour off and reserve the fat. Place the pan over the stovetop burner on medium-low heat. Add the wine, mustard, and honey and bring to a simmer, scraping up any browned bits. Stir together the water and cornstarch, then stir this slurry into the sauce, whisking until thickened, about 1 minute. Whisk in a tablespoon of the reserved pan fat in a slow stream, and season the sauce to taste with salt and pepper.

6 Slice the meat between the ribs; it should be rosy and medium-rare. If you prefer more well-done meat, you can slice between the ribs, arrange them in a single layer in the roasting pan, roast for a few more minutes, keeping an eye on them, and pull them out when they're as done as you want.

7 Arrange the ribs and roasted shallots on a platter and pour the pan sauce and some of the reserved fat over the roast. Season to taste with additional salt and pepper and garnish with the remaining 3 rosemary and thyme sprigs.

top-crusted cottage pie

SERVES 8
ACTIVE TIME: 40 MINUTES
TOTAL TIME: 2 HOURS

Oh, I wish for simpler times, when we could focus on things like the great cottage vs. shepherd's pie debate of 2019 and make it seem like a big deal. This happened over on the *Cravings* site, when we made a yummy ground-beef layer topped with a yummy potato layer and called it shepherd's pie. Well, social media let me know that ground beef = cottage and ground lamb = shepherd, and that I had insulted lamb casseroles and their makers all over the world. Lesson learned, Internet, lesson learned.

So, now I present to you my latest (and, ahem, genius) twist on the genre, which consists of a mega-savory, juicy, meaty layer that holds together between not one, BUT TWO, layers of carbs. It's a literal cottage pie pie—a flaky-creamy-meaty wedge that would be at home in any cottage and has found a permanent home in mine. I used a refrigerated roll-out pie dough because you're already making the meat and tater layers, so why not gift yourself some time back? But if you have time and want to, feel free to make my crust recipe from my first cookbook, or from cravingsbychrissyteigen.com!

3 tablespoons olive oil

1½ pounds ground beef

1½ teaspoons kosher salt, plus more for seasoning

¾ teaspoon freshly ground black pepper, plus more for seasoning

1 small onion, finely diced

1 celery stalk, finely diced

1 medium carrot, diced

3 garlic cloves, minced

¼ teaspoon cayenne pepper

¼ cup tomato paste

3 tablespoons flour

2 cups low-sodium beef broth

2 teaspoons low-sodium soy sauce

1 teaspoon fish sauce

½ cup frozen peas

¼ cup chopped fresh cilantro

1 jumbo or 2 medium russet potatoes (1¼ pounds total)

3 tablespoons unsalted butter

3 tablespoons whole milk

1 (½ a 14-ounce package) refrigerated rollout pie crust (I swear by Pillsbury)

Cooking spray, oil, or butter, for greasing

1 egg, lightly beaten

RECIPE CONTINUES

1 Heat a 9- or 10-inch skillet over medium-high heat. Add 1 tablespoon of the olive oil and the ground beef and cook, adding ½ teaspoon salt and ¼ teaspoon pepper and using a wooden spoon to break up the meat, until it is browned through and no longer pink, 5 minutes. Once done, transfer the meat and any juices to a medium bowl.

2 Add the remaining 2 tablespoons olive oil to the skillet, then add the onion, celery, and carrot and cook, stirring often, until the vegetables soften and the onion is translucent, 6 to 7 minutes. Add the garlic, ½ teaspoon salt, ¼ teaspoon pepper, and the cayenne and cook, stirring, 1 to 2 minutes. Add the tomato paste and cook, stirring, 1 minute.

3 Return the meat and any juices to the skillet and stir to combine with the seasonings. Add 2 tablespoons of the flour and cook, stirring, until absorbed into the meat, 1 minute. Add the broth, soy sauce, and fish sauce. Simmer over low heat, stirring occasionally, until the liquid thickens, 30 minutes. Remove the meat mixture from the heat and stir in the peas and the cilantro; let cool for 20 minutes.

4 While the meat is cooking, wrap the potato (individually, if using 2 smaller potatoes) in damp kitchen or paper towels, trying to make sure they are somewhat sealed (you can rest them in the microwave where they're folded to hold them down). Microwave on high until the potatoes can easily be squeezed and feel cooked through, 14 minutes for 1 jumbo or 10 minutes for 2 medium. Use an oven mitt to remove from the microwave, let cool for 5 minutes, slit open, then scoop the flesh into a bowl; discard the peels. Add the butter and milk, and mash with a fork until smoothish. Add the remaining ½ teaspoon salt and ¼ teaspoon pepper.

5 Preheat the oven to 400°F. Remove the pie dough from the fridge to warm to room temperature for 10 minutes.

6 Spray the bottom and sides of a deep-dish pie plate with cooking spray or grease it with some oil or butter, then spread the potato mixture in an even layer across the bottom of the pie plate. Top with the meat mixture, spreading it evenly.

7 Sprinkle the remaining tablespoon flour on a clean work surface and roll out the pie dough, rolling from the center out to form a 12-inch round. Arrange the pie dough on top of the pie, then fold the edges under to form a ½-inch-thick border and press it into the sides of the pie plate. Crimp the edges with a fork. Use a paring knife to cut a ½-inch hole in the center of the pie. Whisk the egg with a pinch of salt and brush the pie all over with the beaten egg. Arrange the pie plate on a baking sheet to catch any drips and bake until the crust is deep golden and you can see the filling bubbling up from inside, 30 to 35 minutes.

8 Remove the pie from the oven, let it rest 10 minutes, then cut into wedges and serve hot or warm.

john's pan-caribbean oxtail stew

SERVES 6 TO 8
ACTIVE TIME: 35 MINUTES
TOTAL TIME: 4 HOURS

Our love's worth waiting for
Just let it stew some more
Bring out each flavor and spice ...
I can't help that I'm a
sloooowwwwwwww cooker

JOHN: Okay, I really, really, really love slow cooking. I even wrote a song about it and included it on my album *Bigger Love*. The song is also about sex, but let's not change the subject.

This Caribbean staple is spicy, hearty, beefy, and rich. Make sure you start it early and let it sloooooowwwwwwww cook until the meat is starting to fall off the bone, and then watch your lover's clothes fall off their skin. Was that too much? Sorry. Enjoy your stew.

(Alt treatment of this headnote is full of oxtail/oxtale/oxtell puns. It's right up Chrissy's alley. She loves puns: Let me oxtell you an oxtale about the greatest oxtail you ever will eat. Chrissy will love this. This will probably get me laid faster than my song or my stew.)

CHRISSY

What in the f*ck is this lol

ADEENA

NO IDEA

4 pounds (2-inch-thick) oxtail pieces

2 teaspoons kosher salt, plus more for seasoning

Freshly ground black pepper

5 tablespoons olive oil

2 large russet potatoes, peeled and cut into large chunks

4 medium carrots, cut into ¼-inch coins

2 celery stalks, sliced

6 garlic cloves, minced

3 tablespoons tomato paste

2¼ cups dry red wine

2 cups beef broth (regular or low-sodium)

1 (28-ounce) can whole tomatoes, with juice

2 (14-ounce) cans butter beans or lima beans, drained

1 (10-ounce) bag frozen peas

1 tablespoon light brown sugar

2 whole Scotch Bonnet chiles

1½ teaspoons ground allspice

1 teaspoon grated nutmeg

2 beef bouillon cubes

½ teaspoon ground cloves

Hot cooked rice, for serving

1 Pat the oxtails dry and season generously with salt and pepper. In a heavy, large (at least 8-quart) Dutch oven, heat 3 tablespoons of the olive oil over medium-high heat. Sear the oxtails, in batches if necessary, until browned on all sides, turning a few times, about 10 minutes total per batch. Transfer the oxtails to a plate.

2 Add the remaining 2 tablespoons olive oil to the Dutch oven, then add the potatoes, carrots, celery, and garlic and cook, stirring and scraping the bottom to release any browned bits from the pot, until the carrots and celery begin to soften, about 5 minutes. Add the tomato paste and cook, stirring, until caramelized, 2 minutes.

3 Add the wine, broth, and tomatoes, breaking up the tomatoes into pieces with a spoon. Add the beans and peas, brown sugar, chiles, allspice, nutmeg, bouillon cubes, cloves, and 2 teaspoons salt. Bring to a boil. Add the oxtails with any accumulated juices, then reduce the heat to a simmer, cover, and cook until the meat is tender and can be pulled off the bone with a fork, 2¼ to 3 hours. (Check on it once in a while to make sure the liquid hasn't cooked away entirely; you want to end up with a gravy consistency for the sauce.)

4 Uncover, and season to taste with more salt. If the stew feels too liquidy, uncover and boil over high heat to reduce the sauce. Serve with the rice.

lamb & feta
smashburgers

SERVES 4
ACTIVE TIME: 20 MINUTES
TOTAL TIME: 30 MINUTES

A smashburger is a very good thing. But a lamb smashie? With feta? Epically good. If you've ever had your doubts about lamb (and I can't blame you, 'cuz I've been on that very long fence myself), let this be your gateway meal. The salty cheese, a little herby mayo, and sharp raw onions disguise any possible funk. And, ohhh, when the patties hit that sizzling skillet, the feta melds with the hot surface, creating a crunchy crust that will haunt your dreams (in the good way).

¼ cup mayonnaise

¼ cup plain whole-milk Greek yogurt

3 teaspoons finely chopped fresh oregano

1 teaspoon kosher salt, plus more for seasoning

½ teaspoon freshly ground black pepper, plus more for seasoning

1 pound ground lamb

½ cup (2 ounces) crumbled feta cheese

¼ cup finely chopped red onion

2 tablespoons olive oil

1 jalapeño pepper, minced

3 or 4 garlic cloves, minced

4 (⅛-inch-thick) slices red onion

4 brioche or potato hamburger buns, split into halves

4 lettuce leaves

1 medium tomato, cut into 4 slices

1 In a small bowl, whisk the mayo, yogurt, and 1 teaspoon of the oregano, then season to taste with salt and pepper. Cover and refrigerate until ready to use.

2 In a large bowl, use your hands to gently combine the lamb, feta, chopped onion, 1 tablespoon of the olive oil, the jalapeño, garlic, remaining 2 teaspoons oregano, 1 teaspoon salt, and ½ teaspoon pepper. Try to do this until the mixture is just mixed; overworking can make it a bit tough.

3 Divide the mixture into 4 equal balls. Heat a large cast-iron skillet over medium heat, then add the remaining tablespoon olive oil and swoosh it around. Add the burgers, then press them with a spatula into patties. (This is why they're called smashburgers!)

4 Cook the burgers, gently pressing occasionally, until the undersides are deeply browned and crisp, 3 to 4 minutes. Flip with a spatula and cook until the other sides are deeply browned and crisp, another 3 to 4 minutes. Transfer to a plate and cover to keep warm.

5 Add the sliced onions to the skillet and cook until charred and wilted, 3 to 4 minutes, then transfer to the plate with the burgers. In 2 batches, place the buns, cut side down, in the skillet, and toast until golden in parts, 1 to 2 minutes.

6 Spread 1 tablespoon of the mayo-yogurt mixture on each side of each bun, then add a piece of lettuce, an onion slice, and a tomato slice to each bun. Top each with a burger patty, then close the buns. Serve immediately.

pork tenderloin

with rosemary–apple cider sauce

SERVES 4
ACTIVE TIME: 35 MINUTES
TOTAL TIME: 50 MINUTES (INCLUDING MARINATING TIME)

This juicy sliced pork loin dinner cooks super fast but packs in the flavor. A little apple cider and cider vinegar in the pork can put me in the cozy fall zone of mittens, foliage, and contested election results any day of the year. The concept of building a pan sauce out of the stuff that sticks to the bottom of the skillet—known as *fond* in quarters far cheffier than these—shows up all over this book, because it's so GD easy and so effective. Cook your meat, splash in that broth, add a tiny bit of butter, and that's that. Serve alongside the Wilted Kale with Apples & Bacon (page 104), and you're good to go!

1 pork tenderloin (about 1¼ pounds), cut into ½-inch-thick slices

4 tablespoons olive oil

6 tablespoons apple cider or apple juice

1 large fresh rosemary sprig

3 garlic cloves, thinly sliced

½ teaspoon kosher salt, plus more for seasoning

¼ teaspoon freshly ground black pepper, plus more for seasoning

⅓ cup low-sodium chicken broth

1 tablespoon maple syrup

1 teaspoon apple cider vinegar

1 teaspoon cornstarch

3 tablespoons cold unsalted butter, cut into 3 pieces

1 Place the sliced pork tenderloin in a wide bowl with 1 tablespoon each olive oil and apple cider, the rosemary sprig, garlic, ½ teaspoon salt, and ¼ teaspoon pepper. Let it sit on the counter for 15 minutes for a quick marinade (or you can skip the 15 minutes and still get to Flavortown).

2 Heat 2 tablespoons of the olive oil in a heavy 10- to 12-inch skillet over medium-high heat. Scrape the garlic and rosemary off the pork and reserve, then add the pork to the skillet, seasoning it to taste directly with salt and pepper and cooking until browned and just cooked through, 3 minutes per side. Remove from the heat and transfer to a plate. Cover to keep warm.

3 In a small bowl, mix the broth, remaining 5 tablespoons apple cider, the maple syrup, vinegar, and cornstarch.

4 Place the skillet over medium heat, add the remaining tablespoon of olive oil, then add the reserved garlic and cook, stirring, until softened, 1 minute. Add the sauce mixture to the skillet along with the reserved rosemary sprig and bring to a boil, scraping the bottom of the skillet to release any browned bits. Let the sauce reduce and thicken for 2 to 3 minutes, then add the butter 1 tablespoon at a time, whisking it in (you will see the sauce lighten and get creamier with the addition of each piece of butter).

5 Season to taste with salt and pepper, then return the pork and any accumulated juices to the skillet to warm in the sauce for 1 minute. Transfer to a plate, sauce and all.

grilled pork chops with old-school marbella sauce

SERVES 2
ACTIVE TIME: 30 MINUTES
TOTAL TIME: 1 HOUR 40 MINUTES
(INCLUDING MINIMUM MARINATING TIME)

Way back before yours truly was even born, there sat a little gourmet shop in Manhattan, The Silver Palate, where people went crazy for a dish called Chicken Marbella. We're talking viral-before-the-Interwebs nuts, as in people were sharing Xerox copies (maybe you even have no idea what those are?), mailing the recipe to friends, begging their local paper to print it—anything to make this killer marinated chicken with dried fruit and a tangy-sweet sauce.

When the *Silver Palate Cookbook* came out in 1982, *everyone* (more than 2 million to date!) bought a copy, in large part to re-create that recipe, and it still stands the test of time almost forty years later. We made a grilled pork chop with a faster sauce inspired by the original that you can put on any protein you like!

2 bone-in, center-cut pork loin chops (about 1½ pounds total, about 1 inch thick)

4 tablespoons olive oil

3 tablespoons thinly sliced garlic

6 fresh thyme sprigs, plus a pinch of thyme leaves, for garnish

1½ teaspoons kosher salt

¾ teaspoon freshly ground black pepper

10 dried apricots, halved

1 cup low-sodium chicken broth, plus more as needed

½ cup dry white wine

6 pitted prunes

¼ cup pitted green olives, such as Castelvetranos, halved

2 tablespoons capers, drained

2 tablespoons light brown sugar

1½ teaspoons red wine vinegar

¼ teaspoon red pepper flakes

1 Combine the pork chops in a wide bowl with 2 tablespoons of the olive oil, half of the sliced garlic, 3 thyme sprigs, and the salt and pepper. Cover and let sit on the counter for up to 1 hour, or refrigerate for up to 24 hours.

2 Place the apricots in a small saucepan with the chicken broth, bring to a boil over medium-high heat, reduce the heat to medium-low, and simmer until the apricots begin to soften, about 5 minutes. Remove from the heat and let soak for 30 minutes.

3 Heat the remaining 2 tablespoons olive oil in a small saucepan over medium-low heat. Add the remaining garlic and cook, stirring, until fragrant, 2 to 3 minutes. Raise the heat to medium-high, add the wine, let it come to a boil, and reduce by half, 3 to 4 minutes. Add the apricots and the chicken broth along with the prunes, olives, capers, brown sugar, vinegar, red pepper flakes, and the remaining 3 thyme sprigs. Bring to a boil, then reduce the heat to medium-low and simmer, uncovered, stirring occasionally, until the liquid thickens and has reduced to about 1½ cups, 13 to 14 minutes. Discard the thyme sprigs.

4 While the sauce is simmering, heat a grill or grill pan over medium-high heat. Scrape the garlic and thyme from the pork. Cook until grill marks form and the meat is done to just under medium (about 130°F near the bone, if using a meat thermometer), 5 to 6 minutes per side. Let rest for 5 minutes, then serve the chops with the sauce. Garnish with the thyme leaves.

orange chicken

fried-chicken sandwiches

MAKES 4 SANDWICHES
ACTIVE TIME: 45 MINUTES
TOTAL TIME: 1 HOUR 30 MINUTES
(INCLUDING MINIMUM MARINATING TIME)

Oh, excuse my language, but I'm honestly so f*cking excited to write about this one! The stickiness, the crispiness, the sweet, the tart, the slaw. EVERYthing about this sandwich is perfect.

To be honest, I'm guessing you guys don't make a lot of sandwiches from recipes. I rarely get sent pictures of them. My guess is that it's just so damn easy to just make your favorite sandwich, or to hit up a drive-thru to achieve your sammy desires. And it is!! But you also need to trust the fact that when I, an AVID sandwich eater, *love* a sandwich, it means: It. Is. Legit.

The funniest part of this sandwich is that it led to a heated conversation about orange chicken, a dish I LOVE, which I learned John (and his brother!) DO NOT LIKE. I wasn't aware people didn't like orange chicken. It's a Panda Express world and we are just living in it! I actually call restaurants before I order their orange chicken, to make sure it's fried and not grilled; grilled orange chicken is a waste of my precious time. Anyhow, phew. This freakin' sandwich is exactly what a sandwich should be: a Panda Express knockoff in a bun.

Chicken

1 tablespoon low-sodium soy sauce

1 tablespoon fresh orange juice

1 teaspoon finely grated orange zest

½ teaspoon toasted sesame oil

1 large garlic clove, minced

4 (4- to 5-ounce) skinless, boneless chicken breasts or thighs

½ cup flour

2 eggs, lightly beaten

1 cup panko bread crumbs

Paprika

Kosher salt and freshly ground black pepper

Orange Sauce

1 tablespoon cornstarch

½ cup unseasoned rice vinegar

½ cup honey

3 tablespoons orange juice

1 teaspoon finely grated orange zest

1 tablespoon Thai chili-garlic sauce

1 tablespoon light soy sauce

1½ teaspoons toasted sesame oil

1 tablespoon vegetable oil

2 large garlic cloves, minced

Slaw

⅓ cup Kewpie or regular mayonnaise

1½ teaspoons hot Chinese mustard, or 1 tablespoon Dijon mustard

½ teaspoon toasted sesame oil

¼ teaspoon kosher salt

2 cups shredded green cabbage

¼ cup shredded carrot

¼ cup thinly sliced red onion

Vegetable oil, for pan-frying

4 potato or brioche buns, halved and lightly toasted

Fresh cilantro leaves

1 PREPARE THE CHICKEN: In a small glass baking dish, medium bowl, or zippered plastic bag, combine the soy sauce, orange juice, orange zest, sesame oil, and garlic. Add the chicken and toss or smoosh around to coat well. Leave on the counter to marinate for 1 hour, or in the fridge for up to 24 hours.

2 Place the flour in one shallow bowl, the eggs in another, and the panko in a third bowl. Season the flour and eggs with pinches of paprika, salt, and pepper. Remove the chicken from the marinade and dip it in the flour (shake off the excess), then the egg (let the excess drip off back into the bowl), then into the

RECIPE CONTINUES

panko, pressing down so the bread crumbs stick to the chicken. Let the chicken sit while you make the sauce and slaw; this helps everything stick when you fry it!

3 **MAKE THE SAUCE:** In a bowl, dissolve the cornstarch in the vinegar, then stir in the honey, orange juice and zest, chili-garlic sauce, soy sauce, and sesame oil until the honey is dissolved. In a small saucepan, heat the vegetable oil over medium-low heat. Add the garlic and cook, stirring, until fragrant, 1 to 2 minutes. Add the sauce mixture, bring to a boil, reduce the heat to medium-low, and simmer until the sauce thickens, 2 to 3 minutes. Cover to keep warm.

4 **MAKE THE SLAW:** In a medium bowl, whisk the mayo, mustard, sesame oil, and salt in a bowl. Add the cabbage, carrot, and onion and toss to coat.

5 **FRY THE CHICKEN:** Heat ½ inch of the vegetable oil in a large skillet over medium-high heat until very hot but not smoking (a small piece of bread should fry evenly to a nice golden brown when dropped into the oil). Gently arrange the cutlets in the skillet, 2 at a time or all 4 if they can fit without touching, and fry until golden and crisp, 3 minutes per side. Place a few layers of paper towels on a platter and transfer the chicken to them to drain when ready.

6 **ASSEMBLE:** Dip the fried cutlets in the sauce until well coated. Place them on the bottom halves of the buns, pile with some slaw and cilantro, then close with the top halves of the buns. YUM!

juicy chicken paillards
with charred broccolini

SERVES 4
ACTIVE TIME: 35 MINUTES
TOTAL TIME: 1 HOUR 15 MINUTES
(INCLUDING MINIMUM MARINATING TIME)

While I love you and am so, so happy for your friendship, I cannot stress enough how different we are if you love chicken breast. One, I don't like the fact you're outright lying to me, saying it's good. Not liking dark meat and choosing to eat chicken breast is absolutely possible. But just because a choice can be made, it does NOT mean it is a good one.

But, for you, because I love you, we worked very, very hard to make chicken breast great—a pounded, juicy, tender comforter of joy, just for you. We took care of the flavor by marinating it with garlic and lemon. We charred the broccolini to erase any kind of bitterness. We tossed on some blistered cherry tomatoes and finished it all with a garlic-lemon butter sauce. Please enjoy.

1 lemon

4 (4- to 5-ounce) skinless, boneless chicken breasts

6 tablespoons olive oil, plus more for drizzling

5 garlic cloves, thinly sliced

1 teaspoon kosher salt, plus more for seasoning

½ teaspoon freshly ground black pepper, plus more for seasoning

3 or 4 fresh thyme sprigs

1 pound broccolini, ends trimmed

½ cup whole cherry tomatoes

¾ cup low-sodium chicken broth

1 teaspoon finely minced jalapeño pepper, or ¼ teaspoon red pepper flakes

2 tablespoons unsalted butter, chilled

1 Halve the lemon, then cut one of the halves into 4 wedges. Finely grate the zest of the other lemon half and squeeze the juice into a small bowl.

2 Working with 1 chicken breast at a time, place it between 2 pieces of plastic wrap (or inside a large zippered plastic bag) and use the flat side of a meat tenderizer (or an empty wine bottle, or just anything you can whack it with!) and pound until very thin (about ¼ inch thick) but stopping before any holes form in the cutlet. Repeat with the remaining cutlets.

3 Place the chicken in a medium bowl with 2 tablespoons of the olive oil, 3 of the garlic cloves, the lemon zest, 1 teaspoon of the lemon juice, ½ teaspoon salt, ¼ teaspoon pepper, and the thyme sprigs. Gently smoosh around, making sure not to tear those thin cutlets.

4 Let the chicken sit on the counter for 30 minutes or cover and chill/marinate in the fridge for up to 8 hours (if you are pressed for time you can skip this step and the paillards will still be great).

RECIPE CONTINUES

5 Heat a large heavy skillet over high heat. Add the broccolini in an even layer and top with the cherry tomatoes. Cook, not stirring, until the underside of the broccolini begins to char, 2 minutes. At this point, season with the remaining ½ teaspoon salt and add 1 tablespoon olive oil and a generous splash (about ¼ cup) of the chicken broth, which will slightly steam the broccolini and turn it a gorgeous bright green color; cook 1 more minute without disturbing, Flip the broccolini, and cook until it is crisp-tender and the tomatoes are softened, 1 to 2 more minutes.

6 Transfer the broccolini and tomatoes to a plate and cover with foil to keep warm. Rinse and wipe out the skillet.

7 Remove the chicken from the bag, scraping off and discarding the thyme sprigs and garlic slices. Heat the skillet over medium-high heat, then add 1½ tablespoons olive oil. Add 2 of the cutlets to the skillet and cook, seasoning them to taste with salt and pepper, until golden brown and just cooked through, 2 minutes per side. (If you can't fit 2 at the same time without them sitting on top of each other, do this in 4 batches.)

8 Remove the chicken to a plate and repeat with the remaining 1½ tablespoons oil and the 2 cutlets. When finished, add the chicken to the plate and cover with foil to keep everything warm. Add the lemon wedges to the skillet and cook until slightly charred, 2 minutes per side. Add to the plate with the chicken.

9 Let the skillet cool down for a few minutes, reduce the heat to medium-low, then add the remaining 3 garlic cloves and the jalapeño and cook, stirring, until the garlic is softened, 1 minute. Add the remaining ½ cup broth and any juices accumulated on the plate holding the cooked chicken and cook, scraping up all the bits at the bottom of the skillet, until the broth reduces by about half, 2 to 3 minutes. Add 1 teaspoon lemon juice, then remove from the heat and whisk in the butter until you have a dark brown, slightly creamy sauce. Season to taste with additional salt and pepper.

10 Arrange the paillards, broccolini and tomatoes, and lemon wedges on a serving platter. Season to taste with salt and pepper, drizzle with some olive oil, and serve with the sauce.

mother f*ckin' islands-style yaki tacos

MAKES 6 TO 8 TACOS
ACTIVE TIME: 20 MINUTES
TOTAL TIME: 40 MINUTES

I know this recipe name is vulgar, but it's exactly how I speak of this multicultural delicacy. They are not just Yaki Tacos! They are MF Yaki Tacos, and they possess an area in my heart as big as the ones for any of my children (this is almost entirely accurate).

When I lived in Irvine, California, I used to eat these chicken teriyaki tacos at the bar while loosely doing my homework at Islands restaurant. Islands is like a tropical Chili's . . . I think they just spray-paint the same trinkets yellow and green and throw in some surfboards, and bam—decor. Anyway, they're a chain, and I've also eaten these things in Huntington Beach, Las Vegas, Seal Beach, Phoenix, Honolulu. They never, ever fail, and neither will this recipe.

The sauce is SWEET and incredibly salty in a way that punches you in the mouth, but if you're open and ready for it, you WILL fall in love. Oh, my god, I just imagined putting our crispy wonton skins (page 54) on these and had a complete brain freeze at the mere thought of it. Anyhow, what else can I say? They're heaven-sent sweet chicken tacos with pineapple and cheese and a pinch of lettuce—so that makes them healthy!

5 boneless, skinless chicken thighs (about 1½ pounds), cut into 1½-inch pieces

2 tablespoons vegetable or olive oil

1 teaspoon minced garlic

½ teaspoon kosher salt, plus more for seasoning

¼ teaspoon freshly ground black pepper, plus more for seasoning

1 (15-ounce) can pinto beans, drained but not rinsed

½ cup low-sodium chicken broth

½ teaspoon ground cumin

½ cup mayonnaise

2 or 3 drops toasted sesame oil

1 cup (5 ounces) diced fresh or canned pineapple, plus 2 teaspoons pineapple juice

3 tablespoons hoisin sauce

3 tablespoons teriyaki sauce

6 to 8 (6-inch) flour tortillas

1 cup shredded iceberg lettuce

½ cup shredded cheddar cheese

½ cup fresh cilantro leaves

1 large or 2 small avocados, sliced

Lime wedges, for serving

RECIPE CONTINUES

1 In a large bowl, combine the chicken, oil, garlic, ½ teaspoon salt, and ¼ teaspoon pepper. Let the mixture sit out (up to 1 hour) while you get everything else ready.

2 In a small saucepan, combine the beans, broth, and cumin, and bring them to a simmer over medium-low heat. Cook, mashing a few beans here and there with a fork and seasoning to taste with salt and pepper, until the beans and liquid thicken, about 10 minutes. Remove from the heat and keep warm.

3 In a small bowl, whisk together the mayo, sesame oil, and pineapple juice. Season with salt.

4 Heat a large nonstick skillet over medium-high heat. Add the chicken in one layer and cook, without moving, until the underside is golden and caramelized, 5 minutes. Stir the chicken and cook another 5 minutes, until cooked through. Whisk together the hoisin and teriyaki sauces, add to the chicken, lower the heat to medium-low, and simmer, stirring often, until the sauce thickens and the chicken is coated and slightly caramelized, another 2 to 3 minutes.

5 Warm the tortillas by microwaving them for a few seconds or toasting them in a hot, dry skillet, about 10 seconds per side. Build your own tacos by putting some combination of chicken, beans, pineapple, lettuce, cheese, cilantro, and avocado in the tortillas. Dollop with the pineapple-mayo sauce and serve with the lime wedges.

shortcut khao man ghai
(thai chicken & rice)

SERVES 6
ACTIVE TIME: 30 MINUTES
TOTAL TIME: 1 HOUR 30 MINUTES

Readers of my first two cookbooks probably remember a chapter called "Thai Mom," which was about . . . my Thai mom. Well, Pepper's got her own cookbook now, so we said a sad farewell to the "Thai Mom" chapter. Plus, she goes by Yai now, Thai for "grandmother." But don't worry, she is still all over this book!

This is one of a very few, super-select recipes that Mom made for *her* book that I simply had. to. have. in *mine* as well. We actually simplified and tweaked it so it's not quite the same. But it's pure comfort food—clean, poached chicken; rice cooked with the chicken broth that is SO good; and then an amazing ginger-garlic sauce that transports you to Thaitown.

Chicken & Broth

4 bone-in, skin-on chicken thighs

1 (4-inch) piece fresh ginger, halved

10 fresh cilantro stems

1 chicken bouillon cube

1 tablespoon kosher salt

1 carrot, sliced into coins

Rice

3 cups jasmine rice

⅓ cup rendered chicken fat or vegetable oil

10 garlic cloves, minced

1 (1-inch) piece fresh ginger, peeled and cut into 4 slices

1 teaspoon kosher salt

Sauce

¼ cup light miso paste

3 tablespoons low-sodium soy sauce

3 tablespoons light brown sugar

1½ tablespoons white vinegar

10 small garlic cloves

1 (1-inch) piece fresh ginger, peeled and roughly chopped

1 tablespoon fresh lime juice

2 tablespoons low-sodium broth or water

2 radishes, shredded, for serving

1 MAKE THE CHICKEN AND BROTH: Place the chicken, ginger, cilantro stems, bouillon, and salt in a 5-quart saucepan and cover with 12 cups cold water. Bring to a boil, reduce the heat to medium-low, and cook, covered, occasionally skimming off any scum that gathers. After 20 minutes, uncover, add the carrot, and simmer until the chicken is cooked through, another 15 minutes.

2 Remove the chicken from the broth, place it in a large bowl, and cover with ice and water. Chill for 10 minutes, until the chicken is room temperature. Remove the ginger and cilantro from the broth, keeping the carrot in the broth. Measure out 4¼ cups broth for cooking the rice and reserve any remaining broth for serving.

3 MAKE THE RICE: Rinse and swish the rice around in a strainer under cold water until the water runs clear. Drain it well. In a 5-quart pot or Dutch oven, heat the chicken fat or oil over medium heat. Add the garlic and ginger and cook, stirring, until fragrant but not golden, 2 minutes. Add the rice and cook, stirring, until the rice turns shiny and absorbs the oil, 2 to 3 minutes. Add the 4¼ cups reserved broth, reduce the heat to low, cover the pot, and cook the rice, opening and stirring every 4 or 5 minutes, until the rice is tender and the liquid has been absorbed, 19 to 20 minutes; if the rice appears dry, add up to ¼ cup broth.

4 MAKE THE SAUCE: In a blender, combine the miso, soy sauce, brown sugar, vinegar, garlic, ginger, lime juice, and broth and blend until smooth.

To serve, cut the chicken, including the skin, off the bone into slices. Mound about 1 cup of rice onto each serving plate, then add some room-temp chicken. Ladle the remaining broth with some carrots into small bowls, add some shredded radish to the bowls and serve the broth and sauce on the side with the chicken and rice.

skillet chicken marsala

with cauliflower gnocchi & spinach

SERVES 4 TO 6
ACTIVE TIME: 45 MINUTES
TOTAL TIME: 45 MINUTES

If a recipe begins with the word "skillet," you can pretty much bet I'm already on my way to the store. Or at least thinking about the word "skillet." S-K-I-L-L-E-T. Mmmmmm . . .

This is pretty much the restaurant-favorite chicken marsala—sautéed chicken with creamy mushroom-wine sauce, served with spinach and crispy pillows of INTERNET OBSESSION Trader Joe's cauliflower gnocchi. People have devoted whole Instagram accounts and loads upon loads of blogging time to these little pillows; and I gotta say, I was VERY surprised and pleased when I tried them! (Of course, you can use regular gnocchi or another brand of cauli gnocchi—there are some worthy competitors now!)

1 (12-ounce) package cauliflower gnocchi,* thawed if frozen

1½ teaspoons kosher salt, plus more for seasoning

½ teaspoon freshly ground black pepper, plus more for seasoning

1 cup low-sodium chicken broth

2 tablespoons unsalted butter

3 tablespoons cornstarch

1¼ pounds skinless boneless chicken thighs (4 or 5 thighs)

3 tablespoons olive oil

½ cup finely diced onion

5 garlic cloves, minced

8 ounces fresh cremini mushrooms, cleaned, trimmed, and sliced

¾ cup marsala wine

¾ cup heavy cream

¼ teaspoon cayenne pepper

1 (10-ounce) package frozen chopped spinach, defrosted and squeezed of extra liquid

1 Heat a large nonstick skillet over medium heat. Add the gnocchi, season generously with salt and pepper, then pour in ¼ cup broth, cover, and cook until the liquid has been absorbed, 5 minutes. Uncover, then add the butter, tilting the pan to spread it as it melts. Cook until the underside of the gnocchi is toasty, 2 to 3 minutes, then flip and cook another 2 to 3 minutes. Transfer to a plate.

2 In a bowl or zippered plastic bag, combine the cornstarch, 1 teaspoon salt, and ½ teaspoon pepper. Add the chicken and toss until it absorbs all the cornstarch.

3 Heat the skillet over medium-high heat, then add 2 tablespoons olive oil. Add the chicken and cook until browned and just cooked through, 3 to 4 minutes per side. Transfer to a plate.

4 Add the remaining 1 tablespoon olive oil, reduce the heat to medium, and add the onion. Cook, stirring, until it begins to soften, 5 minutes. Add the garlic and cook 1 minute, then add the mushrooms, season to taste with salt and pepper, and cook until the mushrooms soften, 3 to 4 minutes. Add the remaining ¾ cup chicken broth along with the marsala, cream, cayenne, and remaining ½ teaspoon salt. Bring to a boil, then reduce the heat to low and simmer until the sauce is thicker (but not very thick), 12 minutes. While the sauce is reducing, cut the chicken into strips.

5 When the sauce is reduced, add the chicken strips to the skillet. (If there was any pink in the chicken when you cut it, let the strips simmer for a few minutes to make sure they are cooked through.) Scatter the spinach into the skillet. Add the gnocchi, then shake the skillet to coat everything and warm the spinach and gnocchi through.

*If you can't get cauliflower gnocchi, you can use frozen potato gnocchi. Follow the package instructions for cooking them, then continue with the recipe.

spatchcocked thai grilled chicken
with sticky rice balls & spicy sauce

SERVES 4 TO 6
ACTIVE TIME: 45 MINUTES
TOTAL TIME: 13 HOURS 30 MINUTES
(INCLUDING MINIMUM MARINATING TIME)

You have an insatiable need for chicken recipes, and hey, I get it. Chicken soaks up flavor! It's affordable! It feeds a crowd! And so, I spend my days dreaming up ways to put a new spin on the old bird.

But this one isn't so new. It's a classic Thai style of grilled chicken, marinated to give you pops of spice, garlic, and lemongrass, and we figured out a great way to make it at home, no street vendor required.

Spatchcocking is a technique whereby you take a whole bird and open it up flat (kitchen shears are clutch here). It lets you get the rub all over to really pump up the flavor, and it cuts down on cooking time by a LOT, since cooking something flat is way quicker than cooking something round. And the stovetop–hot-oven combo creates a super-juicy chick.

The classic pairing for this chicken is sticky rice, which you roll up into balls—super therapeutic—that become little handheld sauce soakers for all those chicken drippings. Making sticky rice was always a weekend activity in our house, since Mom would soak the rice for hours, then perform an elaborate steaming process that involves a tulip-shaped aluminum pot and a beautiful bamboo cone. Once I challenged her, Mom got really excited about figuring out how to make the sticky rice in the microwave, and after a little trial and error, she truly nailed it! A shorter soak and 15 micro minutes yield the sticky rice you've always wanted! Bonus: you can use plain old sushi or risotto rice, too. Thank you, Mom!

*You usually need to peel the outer layers of a lemongrass stalk, since it tends to be dry and tough. Take a few layers off until you reach the smooth core. Cut off the root end and then slice the white and light parts as thin as you can.

Chicken

5 tablespoons vegetable oil

3 tablespoons minced garlic

2 tablespoons minced lemongrass*

1 tablespoon fish sauce

1 teaspoon sugar

½ teaspoon cayenne pepper

Grated zest of 1 lime

1 (4-pound) chicken, spatchcocked (see Note, page 177) and patted dry

Kosher salt and freshly ground black pepper

Rice

2 cups Thai sticky rice, sushi rice, or risotto (Arborio) rice

1 teaspoon kosher salt, plus more for seasoning

2 tablespoons water

2 scallions (green and white parts), thinly sliced

Sauce

2 tablespoons fish sauce

1½ teaspoons roasted Thai chili powder or red pepper flakes

1 tablespoon hot water

1 teaspoon tamarind paste or fresh lime juice

RECIPE CONTINUES

1 MAKE THE CHICKEN: In a small bowl, combine 3 tablespoons of the oil, the garlic, lemongrass, fish sauce, sugar, cayenne, and lime zest. Rub the garlic mixture all over the chicken, then place in a baking dish, cover with plastic wrap, and refrigerate for at least 8 hours and up to 24 hours. Remove the chicken from the fridge about 30 minutes before cooking.

2 Preheat the oven to 425°F. In a very large skillet, preferably cast-iron, heat the remaining 2 tablespoons oil over medium-high heat. Season the chicken generously with salt and pepper and arrange the chicken, breast side down, in the skillet and cook, not moving, until the breast skin is crisped and golden, 5 to 7 minutes. Carefully flip the chicken, trying not to tear the skin, and transfer the skillet to the oven. Cook until the chicken leg can be jiggled, the juices run clear, and the skin is a deep, golden crisp, 35 to 40 minutes.

3 WHILE THE CHICKEN IS COOKING, MAKE THE RICE: Rinse the rice for about 30 seconds until it runs clear-ish. Place in a large microwave-safe bowl with the salt, then fill with enough water to just cover. Seal with plastic wrap and microwave on high for 7 minutes. Use oven mitts to remove the bowl from the microwave, carefully open the rice, and stir with a moistened silicone spatula or wooden spoon, adding 2 tablespoons water. Recover tightly with new plastic wrap, then cook another 3 minutes. Remove,

uncover again, stir, then reseal with plastic wrap again and cook until the rice is sticky and tender, another 4 minutes. Remove from the microwave, let rest for 5 minutes, then spread out onto a wooden cutting board to cool (this gets rid of any additional moisture).

4 MAKE THE SAUCE: In a small bowl, combine the fish sauce, chili powder, hot water, and tamarind paste. Set aside.

5 Remove the chicken from the oven, let it rest in the skillet for 10 minutes, then transfer to a cutting board (reserve the juices in the skillet) and cut into 8 pieces. Place the chicken on a serving platter. Drizzle the pan juices and any scrapings from the pan over the chicken, and season to taste with salt and pepper. Cover to keep warm.

6 Moisten your hands and form compact balls with the rice, using ¼ cup rice at a time. Season the rice balls with salt and nestle them between the pieces of chicken. Garnish with the scallions, and serve with the sauce.

Spatchcocking

To spatchcock a chicken, place the chicken breast side down on a cutting board. Use kitchen shears to cut out the backbone of the chicken, starting from the cavity and going up to the neck; freeze the bone in a bag and save for broth. Turn the chicken over and press down firmly on the center of the breast with the palm of your hand to flatten the chicken.

sancocho-inspired chicken & corn stew

SERVES 4 TO 6
ACTIVE TIME: 30 MINUTES
TOTAL TIME: 2 HOURS

This thick pot o' soupy stew with its roots in Central and South America will have you cooing with contentment after you consume bowl after bowl of tender dark-meat chicken and sunny little wheels of sweet corn, carrots, and potatoes.

I leave the skin on and the bones in those thighs because if you think a skinless, boneless thigh resists overcooking, wait till you see just how juicy these stay with all their parts intact. Of course, we eat the skin, but feel free to remove it after cooking. I also snuck a bouillon cube in there because I am on a mission to have MSG be your best friend, and if it's good enough for billions of cooks all over the world, it should be good for us 'Mericans!

6 bone-in, skin-on chicken thighs
(3 to 3½ pounds total)

2 teaspoons kosher salt, plus more for seasoning

1 teaspoon freshly ground black pepper

2 tablespoons vegetable oil

1 medium yellow onion, chopped

5 cups low-sodium chicken broth

4 medium carrots, cut into bite-sized chunks

6 garlic cloves, minced

1 large jalapeño pepper (seeded if desired), chopped

1 teaspoon ground coriander

3 large (2 pounds) russet potatoes, peeled and cut into 1-inch chunks

2 ears corn, each cut into 8 equal rounds,* or 4 mini ears, halved

1 large ripe tomato, cored and chopped, or 1 (14-ounce) can diced tomatoes, drained

1 cup chopped fresh cilantro leaves and tender stems

1 chicken bouillon cube
(or 2, if you're salty like me)

1 Pat the chicken dry and season with 1 teaspoon salt and ½ teaspoon pepper. In a large, heavy Dutch oven or soup pot, heat the oil over medium-high heat. Add the chicken in a single layer, skin side down, and brown without moving until the chicken releases easily from the pan, 6 to 7 minutes. Flip and brown an additional 4 minutes, transfer to a plate, then drain all but 2 tablespoons of the fat into a small bowl (save the rest for Mom's Shortcut Khao Man Ghai, page 170).

2 Reduce the heat to medium, add the onion, and cook, without stirring, until light golden, 4 to 5 minutes. Deglaze with ¼ cup of the broth, scraping any browned bits from the bottom of the pot. Add the carrots, garlic, jalapeño, and coriander and cook, stirring occasionally, until the carrots begin to soften, 3 to 4 minutes.

3 Add the potatoes, corn, tomato, ½ cup of the cilantro, and the remaining 4¾ cups broth. Crumble the bouillon cube into the pot along with the remaining teaspoon salt and ½ teaspoon pepper, then nestle the chicken back into the pot along with any juices from the plate. Bring to a boil over medium-high heat, then reduce the heat to low and simmer, covered, until the vegetables are very soft, some of the potatoes are falling apart a bit, and the liquid has thickened, about 1½ hours. Uncover and let cool for 10 minutes.

4 Ladle into bowls, then garnish with the remaining cilantro.

*To cut the corn on the cob, take a long serrated knife and carefully saw the corn into rounds.

greek-ish
roast chicken with potatoes & feta

SERVES 4 TO 6
ACTIVE TIME: 30 MINUTES
TOTAL TIME: 2 HOURS 15 MINUTES

Okay, okay, I listened, and I get that you want a pretty, picture-perfect boobs-up bird you could bring to the table and show off like the domestic gods and goddesses that you are. So here she is.

To season the chicken, I added a cool technique for making a garlic paste to rub all over, which helps prevent the garlic from burning and, in case you missed the middle of this sentence, means you have garlic rubbed all over the chicken. The chicken then gets roasted on a bed of veggies and potatoes and—surprise!—feta, the cheese with whom I've finally entered into a nice sort of friends-with-benefits relationship. Feta is salty. Feta is creamy. Feta is (there, I said it) tasty. And when roasted with the chicken, its flavor melds with the chicken juices and the sauce bursts with tomato goodness and, ohhh, baby. It's ON.

1½ pounds baby potatoes

1½ cups cherry tomatoes

1 small red onion, cut into 8 wedges

22 garlic cloves (yes, for real; it's about 2 whole heads)

7 tablespoons olive oil

3 teaspoons kosher salt, plus more for seasoning

1 teaspoon freshly grated black pepper, plus more for seasoning

1 (8-ounce) block feta cheese, cut into 2 pieces

8 sprigs fresh oregano

¼ teaspoon cayenne pepper

1 large lemon

1 (4½-pound) chicken, patted dry

1 Preheat the oven to 375°F.

2 Place the potatoes, cherry tomatoes, onion, and 10 of the garlic cloves in a medium (10 × 15-inch) roasting pan and toss with 3 tablespoons of the olive oil and ½ teaspoon each of the salt and pepper. Nestle the feta among the vegetables.

3 Chop 9 of the garlic cloves (for about 3 tablespoons) on a cutting board, then sprinkle 2 teaspoons of the salt on top. Cover the garlic and salt with the wide part of a large chef's knife and apply pressure to grind the salt into the garlic a few times, scraping up the mixture and doing it again until a paste is formed. Transfer the garlic paste to a small bowl and add 3 tablespoons of the olive oil, 1 sprig of oregano, the remaining ½ teaspoon pepper, and the cayenne. Zest the lemon straight into the bowl, then stir the paste until all is well combined.

4 Halve the zested lemon. Season the inside of the chicken generously with salt and pepper, then stuff the inside with the remaining 3 garlic cloves, one of the zested lemon halves, and 3 of the oregano sprigs. Rub the paste all over the chicken, then tie the legs together with kitchen twine, if you like! Nestle the chicken among the vegetables in the roasting pan, trying not to have it sit directly on top of the potatoes. Drizzle the remaining tablespoon olive oil over the feta and add the other zested lemon half. Nestle in the remaining 4 oregano sprigs around the chicken and roast, breast side up, until the skin is crisped and golden, the feta is browned, and the potatoes are fully cooked and browned in parts—start checking at 1 hour 30 minutes.

5 Remove the pan from the oven, let the chicken cool for 10 minutes, then snip the string on the drumsticks and remove the oregano, garlic, and lemon half from the cavity (save the lemon!). Cut the chicken into pieces and serve it with the roasted feta and veggies. Season to taste with salt and pepper and squeeze the lemon halves onto the chicken and veggies, if desired.

cheesy turkey rollup
with creamy pesto sauce

SERVES 4 TO 6
ACTIVE TIME: 40 MINUTES
TOTAL TIME: 1 HOUR 25 MINUTES

I am one (secretly) sentimental mama, and my favorite recipe of all time is the Boursin Chicken that first appeared on my old blog, and then in my first book. I love it because you loved it; it was one of those recipes I obsessed over until it was just so, and your responses back then gave me confidence as a cook and made me feel like I had what it took to make recipes that could stand up to your critiques. And I still make it *allll* the time. After making it again one day, I thought to myself, *Would it be crazy to just put it in the next book again?* That way, anyone who had never tried it could enjoy it as much as I do.

Instead, we came up with this turkey rollup, which has major Boursin Chicken vibes but with a whole new spin and look—and the addition of sun-dried tomatoes, mozzarella, pesto, and a two-minute salad on the side that makes this feel like a fancy restaurant dinner. When I turned the recipe from blog to book back in the day, I was still just the right amount of insecure, so I felt the need to re-create the flavors of Boursin with real goat cheese and a bunch of spices and herbs. But now, five years later, I just decided to go back to the source, because Boursin is delicious, perfectly seasoned, and creamy to the max. There really is nothing more perfect than loving you for being you, and that goes for packaged cheese, too. And this concludes my graduation speech.

2 (5.2-ounce) packages Boursin Garlic & Fine Herbs cheese, at room temperature

1 cup (4 ounces) shredded mozzarella cheese

¾ cup thinly sliced fresh basil

¼ cup oil-packed sun-dried tomatoes (about 5), drained and finely chopped

½ teaspoon red pepper flakes

Kosher salt and freshly ground black pepper

1 (1¼-pound) boneless, skin-on turkey breast, or a REALLY big (1¼-pound) boneless chicken breast

6 tablespoons olive oil

½ cup heavy cream

⅓ cup basil pesto (recipe follows; if store-bought, try for refrigerated— the color is brighter and the flavor is fresher!)

2 tablespoons unsalted butter, cut into 4 pieces

2 cups (about 10 ounces) cherry tomatoes, halved

RECIPE CONTINUES

AKES ABOUT 1 CUP
ACTIVE TIME / 5 MIN
TOTAL TIME / 5 MIN

2 cups fresh basil leaves
⅓ cup pine nuts

3 garlic cloves, minced
1 cup finely grated Parmigiano-Reggiano cheese
½ cup extra-virgin olive oil
Salt and freshly ground black pepper

..., pepper,
...y, then unmold them by slipp...
...the cups and gently transferring them t...
...ate. Serve the ham cups with the salad on the side.

Pulse the basil, pine nuts, garlic, and Parm in a food processor 15 times. Turn on the processor and add the oil in a slow, small stream. Scrape down the sides of the bowl if necessary. Season with salt and pepper to taste.

1 Combine the Boursin, mozzarella, ½ cup of the basil, the sun-dried tomatoes, and red pepper flakes in a medium bowl. Season to taste with salt and pepper.

2 Preheat the oven to 350°F.

3 Working from the widest part of the breast, butterfly the breast by cutting into the center until you can open it into something resembling a heart (you want to keep the breast as whole as possible). Keeping the skin side down, place the breast between 2 pieces of plastic wrap and pound to an even ¼-inch thickness (about 12 × 10-inch rectangle). Trim any raggedy ends off the breast and season both sides generously with salt and pepper. Spread the cheese filling in an even layer on top of the turkey, leaving a 1-inch border around the edges. Starting from the narrow end, roll up into a 10-inch-long log. Straighten the skin on top of the log as much as possible, and use kitchen twine (you will need about 5 feet) to tie the log in 4 equally spaced spots, then also tie it the long way once.

4 Brush all sides of the roll with 2 tablespoons of the olive oil and season generously with salt and pepper. Heat 2 more tablespoons olive oil in a 10- or 12-inch heavy oven-safe skillet (such as cast-iron) over medium heat and place the roll, skin side down, in the skillet and brown until golden, tilting the roll to the left and right occasionally so the entire top is golden, 6 to 7 minutes. Flip the turkey skin side up and transfer the skillet to the oven. Roast until

the turkey is golden and a skewer inserted into the center is very hot to the touch (160°F on a meat thermometer, if you have one), 30 to 35 minutes. (Some cheese will probably ooze out and burn in the skillet, and you'll all be fighting for it!)

5 While the roast is cooking, combine the cream and pesto in a small saucepan, bring to a simmer over medium-low heat, and simmer, stirring often, until the sauce thickens slightly, 2 to 3 minutes. Season to taste with salt and pepper, then remove from the heat and cover to keep warm.

6 During the last 10 minutes of roasting, open the oven and place the pats of butter on the top of the turkey. Later, when it's done cooking, remove the turkey from the oven and let rest for 10 minutes, occasionally basting it with pan drippings while it cools.

7 Toss the tomatoes, remaining 2 tablespoons olive oil, remaining ¼ cup basil, and salt and pepper to taste in a bowl.

8 Snip and remove the twine from around the roll and slice the roll into about ¾-inch-thick pieces. Serve the turkey roll, drizzled with the pesto sauce, with some cherry tomato salad on the side.

BASIL PESTO
MAKES 1 CUP

Okay, so this actually *is* the same recipe from my second book. But it's perfect, so why mess with it?

2 cups fresh basil leaves

⅓ cup pine nuts

3 garlic cloves, minced

1 cup freshly grated Parmigiano-Reggiano cheese

½ cup olive oil

Kosher salt and freshly ground black pepper

Pulse the basil, pine nuts, garlic, and parm in a food processor 15 times. Turn on the processor and add the olive oil in a slow, small stream. Scrape down the sides of the bowl, if necessary. Season to taste with salt and pepper. (Store any leftovers in the fridge.)

bbq chicken & rice bowls

SERVES 4
ACTIVE TIME: 25 MINUTES
TOTAL TIME: 50 MINUTES

If you're anything like us, we are constantly running out of bowls . . . meanwhile, all our big plates go dusty in the cabinet, proving once and for all what the best part of any set of dishes actually is. Probably it's due to the popularity of the bowl meal, where everything you want and need for lunch or dinner is piled into one perfect receptacle. The options are endless, and though bowl meals tend to run to the healthier side, ours is sort of a happy compromise. Yes, it's got loads of roasty veggies and a barbecuey skinless chicken situation, but it's also got buttery rice and my precious, sweet canned baked beans I've been crushing on since my days growing up in Idaho.

Most of this meal (except the buttery rice) is roasted together on a sheet pan, with the onion gussying up the baked beans.

½ cup tomato paste

¼ cup (packed) light brown sugar

1½ tablespoons apple cider vinegar

1 teaspoon Worcestershire sauce

2 teaspoons kosher salt, plus more for seasoning

2 teaspoons freshly ground black pepper, plus more for seasoning

1 teaspoon garlic powder

1 teaspoon onion powder

2 chipotle chiles from a can, finely minced, plus enough of the adobo sauce to equal ¼ cup

4 (5-ounce) skinless, boneless chicken thighs

8 ounces thin green beans (haricots verts) or regular green beans, trimmed

¼ cup olive oil

8 thin carrots, trimmed

2 large red bell peppers, cut into 1-inch strips

2 cups broccoli florets

1 medium red onion, cut into 8 wedges

1 (28-ounce) can country-style baked beans, such as Bush's

4 cups hot cooked long-grain white or brown rice

4 tablespoons unsalted butter

¼ cup thinly sliced scallion greens

1 Preheat the oven to 450°F.

2 In a medium bowl, combine the tomato paste, brown sugar, 1 tablespoon of the vinegar, the Worcestershire, 1½ teaspoons salt, 1½ teaspoons pepper, the garlic powder, onion powder, and 3 tablespoons of the chipotle peppers and sauce. Remove and reserve ¼ cup of this sauce, then add the chicken thighs to the bowl and let them marinate for 15 minutes.

3 Line a large (at least 12 × 18-inch) rimmed baking sheet with aluminum foil. Place the haricots verts in a large bowl, toss with 1 tablespoon of the olive oil, and season to taste with salt and pepper. Arrange in a row at one end of the baking sheet and top with the chicken; discard any excess marinade.

4 Add the carrots, bell peppers, broccoli, and red onion to the bowl that the beans were in, add the remaining 3 tablespoons olive oil and season to taste with salt and pepper. Arrange the vegetables at the empty end of the baking sheet in an even layer. Put the baking sheet in the oven and roast until the chicken begins to sizzle, the carrots soften and char in spots, and the broccoli has lots of black bits, 18 to 20 minutes. Remove from the oven, brush the chicken with the reserved sauce, return it to the oven, and bake for another 3 minutes.

RECIPE CONTINUES

5 While the chicken is baking, warm the baked beans with the remaining tablespoon chipotle and remaining ½ tablespoon vinegar in a medium saucepan over medium-low heat. Season with the remaining ½ teaspoon each salt and pepper and stir occasionally.

6 When the chicken and veggies are cooked, remove the onion to a cutting board, chop, and add to the beans. Cut the chicken into strips.

7 Stir together the hot rice with the butter and scallion greens until the butter is melted. Season to taste with salt and pepper. Scoop 1 cup of the rice and ¾ cup of the baked beans into each of 4 bowls. Divide the vegetables and chicken among the bowls, placing them on top of the rice and beans.

chicken tikka masala

with "garlic naan" pita

SERVES 6 TO 8
ACTIVE TIME: 40 MINUTES
TOTAL TIME: 1 HOUR 25 MINUTES

This creamy, tomatoey, gorgeously fragrant Indian meal (which was apparently actually invented by a Bangladeshi chef in a restaurant in Scotland!) gets the blink-and-it's-gone response in my house.

I know this list of spices seems long, but you can save yourself future work and make multiple batches of the spice blend (just mix up the dry spices, from the garam masala to the cayenne, and keep the blend in a jar) so that you can make this quickly whenever you want it again.

Supermarket pita is usually DOA (dry on arrival) but no match for a slather of butter and garlic, which makes these pitas not just edible but also really tasty and perfect for swiping up the sauce.

GARLIC?

Spice Blend

4 teaspoons ground garam masala

1 tablespoon ground cumin

2¼ teaspoons ground turmeric

1½ teaspoons ground coriander

½ teaspoon cayenne pepper, plus more if desired

Chicken Tikka Masala

1½ cups plain whole-milk Greek yogurt

3 tablespoons finely minced garlic

1½-inch piece fresh ginger, grated on a microplane or very finely minced

4 teaspoons kosher salt, plus more for seasoning

2 pounds skinless, boneless chicken thighs, patted dry and cut into 1½-inch chunks

3 tablespoons ghee, clarified butter, or unsalted butter

1 jumbo yellow onion, finely diced

2 tablespoons tomato paste

1 (15-ounce) can tomato sauce

1 tablespoon sugar

1½ cups heavy cream or half-and-half

½ cup frozen peas, defrosted

½ cup chopped fresh cilantro

Hot cooked basmati rice, for serving

"Garlic Naan" Pita (recipe follows), for serving

RECIPE CONTINUES

1 MAKE THE SPICE BLEND: Combine the garam masala, cumin, turmeric, coriander, and cayenne in a small bowl.

2 MAKE THE CHICKEN: In a large bowl, stir together the yogurt, 1½ tablespoons of the garlic, half the ginger, and 2 tablespoons of the spice mixture. Add 2 teaspoons of salt and stir until smooth. Add the chicken and stir to coat. Cover and chill for at least 30 minutes and up to 6 hours. Remove the chicken from the bowl and discard any excess marinade.

3 Heat 1 tablespoon of the ghee in a large (at least 10-inch) skillet over medium-high heat. Add half the chicken mixture, spacing it apart a bit in a single layer, and brown, not moving the chicken if you can avoid it, for 3 minutes, until golden underneath. Carefully flip and fry another 3 minutes. Transfer the chicken to a plate, then repeat with the remaining chicken, adding a bit more ghee to coat the pan, if necessary. Cover the chicken with foil to keep warm.

4 Reduce the heat to medium, add the remaining 2 tablespoons ghee to the pan, then add the onion and cook, stirring often and scraping the bottom of the skillet to loosen any browned bits, until the onion begins to soften, 4 to 5 minutes. Add the remaining 1½ tablespoons garlic and the remaining ginger and cook, stirring often, until fragrant, 1 to 2 minutes. Add the tomato paste, then stir in the remaining 2 tablespoons of the spice blend. Cook, stirring, until fragrant, 30 seconds.

5 Add the tomato sauce, sugar, and the remaining 2 teaspoons salt, reduce the heat to medium-low, and cook, stirring occasionally, until the sauce darkens and thickens slightly, 10 to 12 minutes. Stir in the cream until evenly combined, and cook until the sauce begins to bubble, 1 to 2 minutes. Gently return the chicken to the skillet and cook for an additional 8 to 10 minutes, stirring occasionally, until the chicken is cooked through and the sauce is thick. Add the peas during the last 3 minutes of cooking. Season with salt and more cayenne to taste, then stir in the cilantro and serve with the rice and the pita.

"GARLIC NAAN" PITA
SERVES 2 TO 4

¼ cup unsalted butter, at room temperature

2 tablespoons roughly chopped garlic

½ teaspoon kosher salt

2 (6-inch) pita breads, split open and halves separated

Preheat the oven to 450°F. In a small bowl, combine the butter, garlic, and salt. Spread one-fourth of the mixture on the insides of each pita half, arrange the pita on a baking sheet, and bake until the pita and garlic are golden in spots and the butter is sizzling, 6 to 7 minutes.

john's curry
chicken thighs

SERVES 6 TO 8
ACTIVE TIME: 40 MINUTES
TOTAL TIME: 2 HOURS 40 MINUTES

JOHN: Let's talk about curry, that flavorful comfort food beloved around the world! But can we talk about it without starting an international food fight? Well . . . that's impossible.

The thing that's controversial about curry is that there are a bunch of really wonderful countries that claim THEIR curry is better than everyone else's. India, Jamaica, Trinidad and Tobago, Thailand, Malaysia, South Africa. I shouldn't have even started *naming* countries because I've clearly left out some great ones, and I have international shows that I'd like to do in the future without getting booed off the stage. But I think I can say that the Indian subcontinent usually gets credit for the origin of curry, and the Brits, in their imperialistic zeal, were involved in spreading it.

After years of touring and tasting, and trying to make my own, this is the slow-cooked chicken curry I like to make. The chicken thighs (with skin and bones for maximum fattiness and flavor!) are seasoned, then seared to a crisp before we add a medley of veggies, herbs, coconut milk, and broth. Then I slow-cook it till the chicken is falling off the bone. Then I serve it to Chrissy, and she forgets all the things I did to piss her off earlier. Mission accomplished!

4 pounds bone-in, skin-on chicken thighs (8 to 9 thighs)

3 tablespoons canola oil

3 tablespoons curry powder

2½ teaspoons kosher salt, plus more for seasoning

1 teaspoon freshly ground black pepper, plus more for seasoning

1 jumbo onion, chopped

6 garlic cloves, thinly sliced

1 teaspoon dried thyme

1 teaspoon paprika

1 Scotch Bonnet chile (don't seed if you like it spicy, as we do), finely minced

2 tablespoons tomato paste

1 (14-ounce) can full-fat coconut milk

1½ cups low-sodium chicken broth

1 dried bay leaf

2 chicken bouillon cubes

3 medium potatoes (1½ pounds)

1 pound carrots, cut into chunks

½ pound green beans, trimmed and halved lengthwise

1 large red bell pepper, chopped

Hot cooked rice, for serving

1 Pat the chicken dry with paper towels. In a large bowl, combine 1 tablespoon of the oil with 1 tablespoon of the curry powder and ½ teaspoon each of the salt and pepper. Add the chicken and toss to coat.

2 In a large skillet or nonstick pan, heat the remaining 2 tablespoons oil over medium-high heat. Add half the chicken, skin side down, and brown until the skin is golden and the fat is rendered, 5 minutes. Flip and cook an additional 4 minutes. Transfer the chicken to a plate and repeat with the remaining chicken, using the fat and juices in the pan to brown the second batch.

3 Drain and discard all but 3 tablespoons of the fat from the skillet. Add the onion and cook, stirring, until softened, 5 minutes. Add the garlic, thyme, paprika, remaining 2 tablespoons curry powder, and the chile and cook, stirring, until the garlic softens slightly and the spices are fragrant, 2 to 3 minutes.

4 Add the tomato paste and cook, stirring, an additional 2 minutes. Add the coconut milk, chicken broth, and bay leaf, then crumble the bouillon cubes into the pot along with the remaining teaspoon salt and ½ teaspoon pepper. Raise the heat to high and bring to a boil.

5 Cut 2 of the potatoes into bite-sized chunks and cut the third one in half. Add the potatoes to the pot along with the carrots, green beans, and bell pepper, then nestle the chicken in the liquid (it's okay if a little of the chicken isn't submerged).

6 Return the pot to a boil, reduce the heat to a simmer, cover, and cook until the liquid thickens, about 1½ hours. Find and transfer the potato halves to a bowl, mash them completely with a fork, then return the mashed potatoes to the pot. Season the curry with more salt to taste, cover the pot (but leave a crack open), and continue to cook until the liquid has further thickened, another 30 minutes. Serve over rice.

john's jerk shrimp

& grilled pineapple salad

SERVES 4
ACTIVE TIME: 40 MINUTES
TOTAL TIME: 40 MINUTES

JOHN: Chrissy and I LOVE the taste of spicy, bold Jamaican jerk. We've had jerk chicken and jerk pork at roadside mom-and-pop spots in Jamaica that rivaled the best Michelin-starred food we've had anywhere. Since we live in L.A. most of the year and there aren't nearly as many Jamaican spots as there are in New York, I've started making my own jerk and curries (see page 192) for us at home. This salad, which features grilled jerk shrimp and pineapple, is spicy, tangy, sweet, and so much fun to make and eat. It's hearty enough to be a meal on its own, but I also will serve it as an appetizer before the chicken curry for a little "Jamaican Night."

1 pound large shrimp, peeled and deveined

⅔ cup canola oil, plus more for the grill or pan

2 teaspoons finely grated lime zest and 5 tablespoons fresh lime juice (from 2 limes)

1 tablespoon jerk seasoning (your favorite brand or from recipe, opposite)

3 tablespoons fresh orange juice

2 tablespoons honey

1 teaspoon kosher salt

1⅓ cups fresh cilantro leaves

½ small jalapeño pepper, stem trimmed (seeding optional)

½ cored fresh pineapple, cut into rings, or 1 (20-ounce) can pineapple slices, drained and patted dry

½ medium red onion, sliced into rings

4 cups baby lettuce mix or spring mix

1 large avocado, cut into chunks

½ cup toasted unsweetened coconut*

*To toast coconut, scatter it on a rimmed baking sheet and bake at 350°F until lightly golden, 6 to 7 minutes. You can also toast the coconut in a dry skillet over medium heat for 5 to 6 minutes, stirring as it begins to turn lightly golden and then transferring it to a plate to prevent burning.

1 Place the shrimp in a large bowl, then toss with 1 tablespoon of the oil, half the lime zest, and the jerk seasoning.

2 In a blender, combine the lime juice and remaining zest, the orange juice, honey, salt, ⅓ cup of the cilantro leaves, the jalapeño, and the remaining canola oil and blend until creamy, 20 to 30 seconds.**

3 Heat a grill or grill pan over medium-high heat. Grease the grill or pan lightly with a little oil, then grill the pineapple and red onion until charred and softened, working in batches if necessary, about 3 minutes per side. Transfer to a cutting board, cool slightly, then chop into bite-sized pieces.

4 Grill the shrimp until they turn pink and the edges are blackened, 2 minutes per side.

5 Arrange the lettuce and remaining cilantro in a bowl, then add the pineapple, onion, avocado, and shrimp. Drizzle with the dressing and sprinkle with the coconut.

**If you don't have a blender, or don't feel like cleaning yours, finely chop the cilantro and jalapeño, then whisk them in a bowl with the lime juice and zest, orange juice, honey, and salt. Drizzle in the oil in a slow stream, whisking vigorously, until the dressing is creamy and emulsified.

JOHN'S JERK SEASONING

MAKES ABOUT ⅓ CUP

1 tablespoon onion powder

1 tablespoon garlic powder

2 teaspoons cayenne pepper

2 teaspoons kosher salt

2 teaspoons freshly ground black pepper

1 tablespoon dried thyme

2 teaspoons sugar

1 teaspoon ground allspice

1 teaspoon paprika

½ teaspoon ground cinnamon

½ teaspoon grated nutmeg

½ teaspoon ground cloves

¼ teaspoon ground cumin

In a bowl, combine all the ingredients until well blended and uniform. The seasoning can be kept in an airtight jar indefinitely, but it loses some flavor after a few months.

tom yum
whole fish

SERVES 2 TO 3
ACTIVE TIME: 30 MINUTES
TOTAL TIME: 1 HOUR 5 MINUTES

This recipe is wild! We made it a few times and it actually got to the point where we were, like, "Whoa, this might have been the actual first time we made something that was TOO flavorful." So, we pulled it back a bit and arrived at this sublime compromise.

This fish has all the amazing flavors of tom yum soup, a top order at Thai restaurants—for good reason. It's a hot-and-sour soup with flavors that just crash all over your mouth (that's a good thing)— lemongrass, makrut lime leaves, chiles, garlic, fish sauce . . . Anyway, we figured we should try to use that flavor base to rub a whole branzino, then stuff it with ginger and garlic before baking. It is so incredibly juicy, and nothing gives me more pleasure than having people flake off every tiny bit of fish with a fork. Plates optional!

The eggplant was a last-minute addition, but once you see how it soaks up the juices and sauce from the fish, and the skin gets nice and crispy, the eggplant might become your favorite part of the entire dish.

Paste

⅓ cup vegetable oil

1½ tablespoons tom yum paste (available in Asian groceries or online)

1½ tablespoons fish sauce

½ teaspoon kosher salt

Fish

1 lemongrass stalk

1 (1½-pound) branzino

½ large shallot, cut into ⅛-inch-thick slices

2 thin slices galangal or fresh ginger

2 makrut lime leaves, spines removed and discarded

3 garlic cloves, thinly sliced

3 fresh cilantro sprigs

1 medium Roma (plum) tomato, cut into 8 slices

½ red jalapeño pepper, seeded and cut into thin strips

1 Japanese eggplant (6 or 7 ounces), cut on the diagonal ¼ inch thick

Kosher salt and freshly ground black pepper

1 **MAKE THE PASTE:** In a small bowl, vigorously whisk the oil, tom yum paste, fish sauce, and kosher salt.

2 **MAKE THE FISH:** Cut the lemongrass stalk in half crosswise at the point where the white creamy part turns dark green;

save the dark green part for tea or your bath. Use the flat side of a knife to smash the white portion a few times, then slice it into 3 or 4 pieces on the diagonal.

3 Pat the fish dry, place it on a parchment-lined tray, then rub the inside of the fish with 2 tablespoons of the paste. Layer the lemongrass, shallot, galangal, makrut lime leaves, ⅔ of the garlic, the cilantro, and the tomato slices inside the fish. Rub the fish on the outside with another 3 tablespoons of the paste, then arrange the remaining garlic slices on top of the fish. Let the fish marinate on the counter for 15 to 20 minutes, if possible.

4 While the fish is marinating, preheat the oven to 425°F. In a medium bowl, toss the eggplant with another 2 tablespoons of the paste and arrange in a single layer on a baking sheet. Arrange the fish on top of the eggplant, then place the jalapeño strips in a decorative pattern on the fish. Cover loosely with aluminum foil and bake until almost cooked through, about 20 minutes.

5 Remove the fish from the oven, raise the oven heat to broil, uncover, then return to the oven and broil 2 to 3 inches from the heat until the eggplant and red pepper begin to char and the fish skin crisps, 5 to 6 minutes. Remove from the oven, season with salt and pepper and serve the fish and eggplant with the vegetables.

panko-parmesan-crusted salmon

SERVES 6
ACTIVE TIME: 15 MINUTES
TOTAL TIME: 35 TO 50 MINUTES

Sheet pan dinners! There are entire cookbooks dedicated to this brilliant concept, and though I tend not to jump on bandwagons, in this case I will happily play every instrument if it means you will make this luscious salmon. The mustardy mayo coating seals all the moisture into the silky fish while creating the ideal bed for the crunchy panko, which bakes up golden, cheesy, and toasty. I'm glad I left room on the pan for the pretty green and yellow zucchini, which make an honest meal out of the fish.

¼ cup Dijon mustard

¼ cup mayonnaise

2 teaspoons honey

1½ teaspoons kosher salt, plus more for seasoning

½ teaspoon freshly ground black pepper, plus more for seasoning

1 cup panko bread crumbs

4 tablespoons olive oil, plus more for brushing the pan

½ cup (1 ounce) finely grated Parmigiano-Reggiano cheese

1 (2½-pound) skin-on salmon fillet

1½ pounds yellow summer squash and zucchini, cut into ½-inch-thick rounds

6 fresh thyme sprigs, plus more for garnish

1 lemon, cut into wedges

1 Preheat the oven to 425°F.

2 In a small bowl, whisk together the mustard, mayo, honey, ½ teaspoon salt, and ¼ teaspoon pepper. In a separate bowl, toss the panko with 2 tablespoons of the olive oil until evenly coated, then toss in the parm and ½ teaspoon salt.

3 Brush a rimmed baking sheet (sheet pan) with olive oil, then place the salmon on the baking sheet. Season the salmon to taste with salt and pepper, then coat the top evenly with the mustard-mayo mixture. Sprinkle the crumbs evenly over the coating.

4 In a large bowl, toss the squash with the remaining 2 tablespoons olive oil, ½ teaspoon salt, and ¼ teaspoon pepper. Arrange the squash around the salmon, and scatter the thyme sprigs on top. Bake until the salmon is done to your liking, 18 to 20 minutes for medium-rare, 21 to 23 minutes for medium, and 24 to 25 minutes for well done, rotating the pan halfway through.

5 Cut the salmon into pieces, divide it among the plates, and put some of the squash on each plate. Season to taste with salt and pepper and garnish with some fresh thyme sprigs. Serve with lemon wedges.

twice-baked
actual
scallop
potatoes

SERVES 2
ACTIVE TIME: 30 MINUTES
TOTAL TIME: 1 HOUR 45 MINUTES

I was kind of shocked I'd never had a baked potato in any of my books because it's a thing of perfection even if you just bake it, split it, and load it with sour cream, cheddar, and bacon (um, BRB). This sexy, simple little meal started out as a semi-joke (get it? "scallop potatoes" instead of "scalloped"???), but it turned out to be something really delicious!

Much of the work—letting the tater bake until soft—is passive, which is kind of like cheating in the best possible way. I love the way you hollow out the potato after it's baked, creating its very own bowl, then reunite the filling with its mama before the second bake. And the spicy, scallop-studded filling and crispy shell? Wow. Use any scallops you can find, or you could use little cubes of fresh salmon or tuna, too.

2 large (12- to 14-ounce) russet potatoes, scrubbed and dried

4 teaspoons vegetable oil

3 tablespoons mayonnaise

¾ cup (1½ ounces) finely grated Parmigiano-Reggiano cheese

1 tablespoon unsalted butter, at room temperature

2 teaspoons Sriracha, plus more as desired

½ teaspoon fish sauce

1 teaspoon unseasoned rice vinegar

½ teaspoon garlic powder

¼ pound sea scallops, cut into ½-inch cubes

3 tablespoons thinly sliced scallion greens

Kosher salt

1 Preheat the oven to 400°F.

2 Prick each potato several times with a fork, then rub each potato all over with 1 teaspoon of the vegetable oil. Place on a baking sheet and bake until the potatoes are soft, 1 hour to 1 hour 5 minutes. Remove from the oven and let cool for 5 minutes.

3 Halve the potatoes and scoop out the flesh, leaving ¼ inch of flesh with the peel intact on the sides and bottoms of the potatoes (discard any skin you removed while scooping). Raise the oven temperature to 440°F.

4 Place the potato flesh in a bowl and mash until almost smooth; you should have about 2 cups. (Save any extra for another use.) To the remainder, add the mayo, parm, butter, Sriracha, fish sauce, vinegar, and garlic powder and mash until smooth. Fold in the scallops and 2 tablespoons of the scallion greens.

5 Brush the inside and outside of each potato skin with 1 teaspoon vegetable oil and season the insides with salt. Stuff one quarter of the filling inside each potato, return the potatoes to the baking sheet, and bake until the scallops are cooked and the tops of the potatoes are slightly browned in parts, 11 to 12 minutes. If desired, remove the potatoes from the oven and set the oven to broil, then broil the potatoes until the tops are more deeply golden, 1 to 2 minutes. Garnish with the remaining scallion greens.

john's
spaniversary
paella

JOHN: As many of you know, after an extremely challenging pregnancy, we lost our little baby Jack on the last day of September 2020. Leading up to that day, Chrissy was doing her best to save his life. Her placenta had abrupted and the doctor said our only hope was for Chrissy to stay on bed rest: Don't move, and maybe things will heal and he could safely grow.

Our anniversary falls on September 14, and I had planned a romantic getaway, but we couldn't do that. When your partner is carrying your child and things are so challenging, it's a very powerless feeling. I wanted to help as much as possible, but there's nothing you can do about the central cause for concern. The best you can do is to be there to support her and make all the other aspects of her life easier, more joyful, in any way you can.

So, I made a plan to cook her a special anniversary meal. We talked about it in the morning and she said she was craving Spanish tapas. So, I set out to fulfill all of Chrissy's desires and "Spaniversary" was born. I made bacon-wrapped dates, ham and cheese croquetas, and gambas al ajillo (garlic shrimp) starters, and the main course was a hearty paella full of spice and bursting with a wonderful combination of rice, vegetables, meat, and seafood. It definitely made Chrissy's night.

Of course, a beautiful meal won't solve all your problems, but it's a good way to show someone you love them. Make this paella for someone you love.

7 cups low-sodium chicken broth

2 tablespoons olive oil

1 pound spicy Spanish-style chorizo sausage links, cut into ½-inch-thick rounds

4 small skinless, boneless chicken thighs (1 pound), cut into bite-sized pieces

2 teaspoons kosher salt, plus more for seasoning

½ teaspoon freshly ground black pepper, plus more for seasoning

1 jumbo onion, diced

1 large green bell pepper, seeded and diced

5 garlic cloves, finely minced

¼ cup tomato paste

1 (14-ounce) can whole tomatoes, with juice

2 teaspoons paprika

1½ teaspoons dried thyme

1 generous pinch of saffron threads (just under ¼ teaspoon)

½ teaspoon cayenne pepper

2¾ cups Calsaparra, Bomba, or Arborio rice (all "round," starchy varieties)

8 jumbo (about 1 pound) shrimp, preferably with peel and head, or 1 pound peeled and deveined large shrimp

¼ cup chopped fresh parsley or cilantro

Lemon wedges, for serving

RECIPE CONTINUES

1 In a medium saucepan, bring the broth to a low simmer, cover, and keep warm on a back burner over low heat.

2 Heat a large (14-inch) cast-iron skillet or other high-sided heavy skillet over medium-high heat. Add the olive oil, swirl it around, then add the sausage and cook, stirring often, until just browned, 2 to 3 minutes. Remove the sausage from the skillet, leaving as much of the oil in the pan as you can.

3 Season the chicken generously with salt and pepper, add it to the skillet, and cook, stirring once, until the chicken is lightly browned, 3 to 4 minutes. Transfer the chicken to the plate with the sausage, again leaving the oil in the skillet.

4 Add the onion and bell pepper and cook, stirring occasionally and scraping the bottom of the pan to loosen any browned bits, until softened, 5 to 6 minutes. Add the garlic and cook, stirring, 1 more minute. Add the tomato paste and cook, stirring, until caramelized, 2 minutes. Add the tomatoes and their juice and cook, breaking up the tomatoes with a spoon and stirring, until some of the liquid is absorbed, 1 to 2 minutes.

5 Stir in the 2 teaspoons salt, ½ teaspoon pepper, the paprika, thyme, saffron, and cayenne, then return the sausage, chicken, and any juices back to the skillet. Add the rice and cook, stirring constantly, until shiny and coated in oil and juices, 2 minutes. Carefully pour in enough of the hot broth to completely cover the rice (5 to 6 cups) and very gently stir and shake the skillet so the broth settles in. Cook the rice, stirring occasionally. Gradually add more broth (you shouldn't need much more than ½ cup more) to keep the rice fully covered for the first 10 minutes.

6 Reduce the heat to medium and continue to cook the paella (DON'T stir!), adding small amounts of broth to cover until a grain of rice is very al dente (not quite edible yet) and most of the liquid is absorbed but some is still visible, 13 to 14 minutes. (You may not use all of the broth.) If you want to develop a soccarat (crust) underneath, rotate the pan around the burner about 90 degrees every minute or so.

7 Arrange the shrimp on top of the rice and cook, uncovered, until mostly cooked through, 4 minutes per side if using head-on jumbo shrimp or 2 minutes per side for smaller, peeled shrimp. Remove from the heat, cover with a lid or foil, and let rest to develop the underside crust and finish cooking the shrimp, about 10 minutes. Uncover and scatter with the parsley.

8 To serve, scoop out portions of the rice and shrimp from the skillet, making sure to scrape the bottom to include the crispy, charred layer of rice on the bottom of the skillet. Do not hog all the soccarat for yourself, as much as you will want to. Serve with the lemon wedges.

date-night cod in spicy tomato butter sauce

SERVES 2
ACTIVE TIME: 30 MINUTES
TOTAL TIME: 25 MINUTES

When I go out for a date night with John, and I see on the menu a poached fish with broth, I know the scent is supposed to waft up into your nose and entrance you. Honestly, John lives for it. Absolutely loves that shit. Me, not so much. I always feel like I go home and eat more. Every single time.

To really satisfy me, I need it to have punchy flavor, and this one has it. A snowy chunk of perfectly cooked cod rests in a buttery, tomatoey, tangy broth, and it's heaven. It fills you up, makes you feel great, and it's simple, beautiful, and eye-catching. Your date's gonna love it.

Now that I'm thinking about it, your kids will love this, too. Wait, what are the kids doing here?? These kids spoil everything—even a date night meal in my mind, goddammit!

2 (6-ounce) skinless center-cut cod fillets (about 1 inch thick)

1 teaspoon kosher salt, plus more for seasoning

2 tablespoons olive oil

2 large shallots, very finely minced

3 garlic cloves, finely minced

3 vine-ripened medium round or 4 Roma (plum) tomatoes, cored and cut into ½-inch dice (about 2 cups)

1 small (preferably red) jalapeño pepper, thinly sliced (seeded, if you must)

½ cup dry white wine

3 tablespoons unsalted butter, chilled and cut into 3 pieces

1 teaspoon white wine vinegar

Fresh cilantro sprigs, for garnish

1 Pat the fish dry with paper towels and season generously on all sides with some salt. Heat a 9- or 10-inch skillet with a lid over medium heat for 2 minutes. Add 1 tablespoon of the oil to the pan, raise the heat to high, wait 30 seconds, then add the fish, top side down, and sear, uncovered, without moving, until the fish develops a little golden color, 3 minutes. Use a fish spatula to remove the fillets to a plate, browned side up, and cover to prevent the fish from drying out.

2 Reduce the heat to medium-low, add the remaining tablespoon of oil, then the shallots, and cook, stirring often, until softened and translucent but not browned, 3 minutes. Add the garlic and cook, stirring constantly, 1 more minute. Add the tomatoes, jalapeño, and 1 teaspoon salt, raise the heat to medium-high, and cook, stirring often, until the tomatoes soften slightly and release some of their liquid, 2 to 3 minutes. Add the wine and bring to a boil over high heat, then reduce the heat to medium and cook, stirring occasionally, until the tomatoes soften further and the liquid reduces a bit, 3 to 4 minutes.

3 Whisk the butter into the skillet 1 piece at a time until you have a lightened, creamy liquid. Stir in the vinegar, then return the fish, browned side up, to the skillet, cover, reduce the heat to medium-low, and cook until the fish is just cooked through, 5 or 6 minutes. Uncover, then divide the sauce and fish between 2 bowls. Season with more salt to taste and garnish with the cilantro.

roasted spaghetti squash

with fresh summer marinara sauce

SERVES 4
ACTIVE TIME: 30 MINUTES
TOTAL TIME: 1 HOUR 30 MINUTES

I'm ashamed of the days I used to think spaghetti squash was an Instagram gimmick. I genuinely thought it was just something that looked cool on social media only. It's squash that naturally looks like spaghetti when you scoop it out. Yay. But THEN I came upon it at Craig's restaurant in Beverly Hills, L.A.'s number-one guaranteed paparazzi haven! (Seriously, you will walk in and randomly sit between Sylvester Stallone's entire family and a meeting between John Mayer and Lisa Vanderpump.) And then I found out that spaghetti squash is a legit good food!!

So, I wanted to give you spaghetti squash with a deliciously light and easy marinara sauce (18 minutes!!) that was full of flavor. Zucchini makes this dish a *dish,* giving it substance, and hearty amounts of onions, basil, garlic, and oregano take it to flavor country. Of course, this isn't actually spaghetti in any way, but it's one of those very rare times where it just doesn't effing matter!

1 large spaghetti squash
(about 3 pounds)

7 tablespoons olive oil

2 teaspoons kosher salt, plus more
for seasoning

Freshly ground black pepper

1 medium onion, diced

3 garlic cloves, minced

½ pound mixed small zucchini
and yellow summer squash, halved
lengthwise, then sliced

2 pounds very ripe tomatoes, cubed

¼ cup shredded fresh basil leaves,
plus more for garnish

1 teaspoon chopped fresh oregano

Freshly grated Parmigiano-Reggiano
cheese, for garnish

1 Preheat the oven to 400°F. Use a large, sharp knife to cut the spaghetti squash in half lengthwise. Use a large spoon to scoop out and discard the seeds. Brush each cut side of the squash with 1 tablespoon of the olive oil and season generously with salt and pepper. Place the squash, cut side down, on a small, rimmed baking sheet or in a 9 × 13-inch baking dish. Use a small paring knife to pierce the tops of the squash 2 or 3 times. Roast until the tops are slightly slumped and can be easily pierced with a fork, about 1 hour.

2 While the squash roasts, heat 2 tablespoons of the olive oil in a medium (at least 3-quart) saucepan over medium-low heat. Add the onion and cook, stirring, until lightly golden, 9 to 10 minutes. Add the garlic and cook 1 more minute. Add the summer squash along with 2 teaspoons salt; season with pepper to taste. Cook until slightly softened, 3 to 4 minutes. Add the tomatoes, bring to a boil, reduce the heat to medium-low, and cook, trying not to break up the tomatoes, until they release their juices, a rustic sauce forms, and some of the liquid is reduced, 17 to 18 minutes. Stir in the ¼ cup basil leaves and the oregano and season to taste with more salt and pepper.

3 When done, remove the spaghetti squash from the oven, flip it over, and use a fork to scrape out and transfer the squash strands to a large bowl. Season the strands with 2 tablespoons of the olive oil and season to taste with salt and pepper. Arrange the squash on a serving platter, top with the sauce, then drizzle the remaining 2 tablespoons olive oil over and garnish with the parm.

chickpea crunch-wraps

SERVES 4 TO 6
ACTIVE TIME: 40 MINUTES
TOTAL TIME: 1 HOUR

I spend many hours of my weekends flipping through magazines, looking at the latest food trends and learning little bits about olive oil, canned tomatoes, truffles, all sorts of things. One thing I recently noticed is America's LOVE of chickpeas, a love I was unaware of! A lot of chickpeas are eaten by vegans and vegetarians, so I wanted to join that mindful, plant-based party while still making something that I could relate to: Taco Bell.

So, here you have it: a veggie crunchwrap! A crunchy taco shell and a soft tortilla, married with a layer of mashed chickpeas and all kinds of veg and cheeses stuffed inside . . . lay six of these bad boys on a long platter and pretend you're driving through on a run for the border. Just do it without meat. And you KNOW I don't do veggie unless it's good. This. Is. Great.

6 (4-inch) taco-sized flour tortillas

6 hard-shell corn taco shells

5 tablespoons vegetable oil

1 medium zucchini, cut into ¼-inch-thick coins

1 red bell pepper, diced

1½ teaspoons ground cumin

1½ teaspoons kosher salt, plus more for seasoning

½ teaspoon cayenne pepper

1 medium onion, diced

3 garlic cloves, thinly sliced

2 (14.5-ounce) cans chickpeas, drained

1 cup low-sodium vegetable broth

¼ cup chopped fresh cilantro, plus whole leaves for garnish

¾ cup (about 3 ounces) shredded Mexican-blend cheese

1 medium avocado, thinly sliced

½ cup sour cream

¼ cup finely diced red onion

Your favorite hot sauce (Cholula)

1   Preheat the oven to 425°F. Fit the flour tortillas inside the hard taco shells to shape them.

2   Heat 2 tablespoons of the oil in a large skillet over medium-high heat. Add the zucchini and bell pepper along with ½ teaspoon cumin, ½ teaspoon salt, and ¼ teaspoon cayenne, and cook, stirring occasionally, until lightly charred and softened, 5 minutes. Transfer to a plate. Add another 2 tablespoons oil to the skillet, then add the onion and cook over medium heat, stirring, until lightly golden, 9 to 10 minutes.

Add the garlic and cook, stirring, for 1 more minute. Add the chickpeas and broth to the skillet, bring to a boil, reduce the heat to medium-low, and simmer, stirring occasionally, until the chickpeas absorb most of the liquid, 10 to 11 minutes.

3   Transfer half (about 2 cups) of the chickpea mixture to a bowl.

4   To the chickpeas in the skillet, add the zucchini mixture and the remaining teaspoon each cumin and salt and the remaining ¼ teaspoon cayenne. Cook, stirring, 1 minute, then add the ¼ cup cilantro and remove from the heat.

5   Mash the chickpeas in the bowl until mostly smooth. Remove the flour tortillas from the hard shells and brush their outsides with the remaining 1 tablespoon oil, then sprinkle with salt. Spread about 3 tablespoons of the mashed chickpeas on the unbrushed side of each tortilla, taking it almost to the edge. Wrap each flour tortilla around a hard-shell corn taco, using the mashed chickpea as "glue."

6   Fill each taco with a heaping ⅓ cup of the filling, then top each with 2 tablespoons of the cheese blend. Stand the tacos up in an 8-inch square baking dish and bake until the cheese is melted, 4 to 5 minutes. Garnish with the avocado slices, sour cream, red onion, and cilantro leaves, and serve with your favorite hot sauce.

super-crunchy tofu ginger stir-fry

SERVES 4
ACTIVE TIME: 30 MINUTES
TOTAL TIME: 30 MINUTES

Look, I'm not known for saying things like "crunchy blocks of golden, shimmering tofu," but I saw them in the pages of *Bon Appétit*, and I decided to get with this particular veggie program, quick.

Sometimes you just need your shrimp/protein/chicken/pork/cardboard to be a vehicle for crunch, and this one delivers faster than Postmates. There's no coating, no dredging, no battering involved—you just pat that soy block dry with some towels, cube it up, heat some oil, and within minutes you've got a surprisingly crispy, tasty delivery system for the ginger-packed, shiny glazy sauce with my love, sweet chili, at its base. I use carrots (love the pop of color they provide!) and snap peas, but by all means do you, and by you I mean broccoli, bell peppers—whatever veg gets the job done.

1 (14-ounce) block extra-firm or firm tofu

¾ cup low-sodium chicken broth

½ cup bottled Thai sweet chili sauce

1½ tablespoons low-sodium soy sauce

¾ cup vegetable or canola oil

Kosher salt

1 tablespoon minced fresh ginger

1 tablespoon minced garlic

3 scallions (whites and greens separated), thinly sliced

1 small red (or green) jalapeño pepper, minced

8 ounces sugar snap peas, ends trimmed and strings pulled

3 small or 2 medium carrots, cut into ¼-inch coins

Hot cooked rice, for serving

1 Place the tofu on a plate, top with another plate, then weight the plate down with a heavy can and let sit for 5 minutes. Drain, then place the tofu between a double layer of paper towels and gently press to absorb any excess liquid. The more liquid you eliminate, the crispier the tofu will be.

2 In a small bowl, combine ½ cup of the broth with the chili sauce and soy sauce.

3 Fold several very absorbent paper towels (or a couple of clean kitchen towels) into a stack on a large plate. Cut the tofu block in half lengthwise, then cut each half into 6 rectangles and cut each rectangle in half again, so you end up with 24 pieces. Lay the tofu between layers of the towels and press down on them for 10 minutes to squeeze out more water.

4 Heat the oil in a large nonstick skillet or wok over medium-high heat until shimmering. Carefully add half the tofu (don't splash yourself!), spread it out in one layer, and cook, shaking the pan occasionally, until well-crisped, 4 to 6 minutes. Use a spider or strainer to transfer the tofu to a paper towel–lined plate to drain and season well with salt. Repeat with the remaining tofu.

5 Transfer all but 2 tablespoons of the oil in the skillet to a glass jar or bowl to cool (reuse it or discard it later!). Return the skillet to medium-high heat and add the ginger, garlic, scallion whites, and jalapeño and cook, shaking the pan, until fragrant, 2 minutes. Add the peas and carrots, then add the remaining ¼ cup of the broth, and cover until the peas turn bright green and the carrots begin to soften, 3 to 4 minutes. Uncover and add the chili-soy mixture, toss with the vegetables, then add the tofu and cook, tossing to coat, until warmed through, 1 to 2 minutes.

6 Serve with hot rice and garnish with the scallion greens.

pad see ew cabbage

with a runny egg

SERVES 3 TO 4
ACTIVE TIME: 20 MINUTES
TOTAL TIME: 25 MINUTES

I know what you're thinking, but there is absolutely NOTHING ew about this dish!!

AHEM, okay, sure, pad thai, tom yum soup, and papaya salad are the usual Thai restaurant orders, but I feel in my SOUL that pad see ew is majorly slept on. The bouncy, smooth noodles, the sweet soy sauce, the crispy, toasty edges, and the whipped egg swirled in—my god, this NEEDS to be in your life if it isn't yet.

Now, of course I could have given you an actual recipe for pad see ew, but honestly, there are plenty online and my mom has an incredible recipe for it in *her* book. But what's NOT out there is those same sweet-savory flavors, tossed and toasted with stir-fried *cabbage*. Beyond just being WAY less carby, I've saved you from the brutal task of finding fresh wide rice noodles, which honestly is next to impossible if you don't have an Asian supermarket nearby. The cabbage still gets that sweet caramelization, plus crunch, and if you'd like, feel free to spice it up with red pepper flakes. Personally, I like to keep it on the sweet side, but good lord, you'll love this either way.

RECIPE CONTINUES

Cabbage

3 tablespoons oyster sauce

2 tablespoons low-sodium soy sauce

1 tablespoon sugar

1 medium head green cabbage
(2½ pounds)

5 tablespoons vegetable oil

1 teaspoon kosher salt

Red pepper flakes (optional)

2 scallions (greens and whites
separated), thinly sliced

3 garlic cloves, thinly sliced

Runny Eggs

Vegetable oil, as needed

4 eggs

Kosher salt and freshly ground
black pepper

1 **MAKE THE CABBAGE:** In a small bowl, whisk together the oyster sauce, soy sauce, and sugar. Cut the cabbage in half through the core, then cut a "V" from the cut side of each half to remove the core, then discard the core. Cut the cabbage halves into 1-inch-wide ribbons and separate them. (You should have 10 to 12 cups of ribbons, but don't worry; it shrinks down.)

2 Heat 4 tablespoons of the oil over medium-high heat in a very large (12- or 14-inch) skillet. Sprinkle ½ teaspoon of the salt right onto the oil, then arrange the cabbage in as much of a single layer as possible in the skillet, cramming on some pieces if you need to. (If you don't have a huge skillet, do it in 2 batches with half the oil and cabbage each time.) Sprinkle the remaining ½ teaspoon salt and the red pepper flakes (if using) on top of the cabbage and cook, uncovered, without stirring, until the underside is charred and caramelized, 4 to 6 minutes. Stir, and then continue to cook, moving the cabbage around, until it's a little more wilted and charred, 5 to 6 minutes.

3 When the cabbage is pretty tender but still has some snap, push it to the side of the skillet, then add the remaining 1 tablespoon oil to the empty side of the skillet. Add the scallion whites and the garlic and cook, stirring, 1 minute, without mixing it into the cabbage. Then stir everything together and add the oyster-soy mixture. Cook, stirring until the cabbage shrinks a bit more, 2 minutes. Remove from heat and keep warm.

4 **MAKE THE EGGS:** Heat a small (8-inch) nonstick skillet over medium-high heat. Add about 3 tablespoons of the oil, let it heat for about 10 seconds, then crack an egg into the skillet and cook, tipping the skillet slightly and using a spoon to baste the white of the egg with the oil, until the edges get lacy and crisp, the white is set, but the yolk is still runny, 2 to 3 minutes. Use a fish spatula or other spatula to carefully transfer the egg to the skillet and place on the cabbage, then repeat with the remaining eggs, adding oil as necessary between batches.

5 Once you get the eggs in the skillet with the cabbage, season them with salt and pepper, then scoop out the egg-topped cabbage onto serving plates. Garnish each with the scallion greens.

mile-high-worthy veggie-stuffed poblanos

SERVES 4
ACTIVE TIME: 30 MINUTES
TOTAL TIME: 1 HOUR 15 MINUTES

If you know me at all, you'll know that I am absolutely b o n k e r s for airplane food. I know you're thinking first class—yes, but no. I legit love ANY airplane meal I, or you, have ever been served. Something about those meals just excites my mind. Even just thinking about how they get made is fascinating—the idea that oilier fish is best in the dry sky, or the science that says food must be saltier for you to taste in high altitude. *Top Chef* once had a challenge (my FAVORITE), whereby the chefs had to create the ultimate airplane meal. Some dishes do nottttt do well in the sky: scrambled eggs (it basically turns into a cut-up sponge!), hot salmon (never: only okay cold on a salad!), steak (good god, no).

Where is this going, you ask?? Well, I want to tell you that this recipe is SO reminiscent of my absolutely favorite kind of in-flight meal—even if you don't share my airplane food kink, it's the kind of dish so full of flavor and color it will wake you up from any mile-high stupor. The soft, roasted poblano chile acts as a nest for an extremely well-curated grouping of veggies (you will fall in love with the cauliflower rice), and you'll very much enjoy sopping up the slightly smoky, sweet-pepper tomato sauce with every single bite.

If you've never had a poblano, they are like green bell peppers' cooler cousins, with thinner skins, prettier color, and a taste that's something like a jalapeño with 95 percent of the spice removed. Blanket these with cheese, bake 'em up, and kiss the sky!

1 (24-ounce) jar good-quality marinara sauce

1 (15-ounce) jar fire-roasted red peppers, drained, rinsed, and drained again (see Note, page 218)

1½ teaspoons kosher salt, plus more for seasoning

4 medium (about 6-inch-long) poblano chiles

3 tablespoons vegetable oil

6 ounces fresh cremini mushrooms, stems removed

1 large carrot

1 medium onion, finely diced

1 tablespoon minced garlic

1 teaspoon finely diced jalapeño pepper (seeded, if desired)

½ teaspoon ground cumin

1 (10-ounce) package frozen cauliflower rice, defrosted and squeezed to remove all extra liquid

1½ cups shredded Mexican-blend cheese

½ cup fresh bread crumbs

½ cup drained canned corn

½ cup chopped fresh cilantro, plus more for garnish

¼ cup crumbled cotija or queso fresco cheese

RECIPE CONTINUES

1 Preheat the oven to 425°F.

2 In a blender or food processor, combine the marinara, roasted peppers, and ½ teaspoon of the salt in a blender or food processor and process until smooth, 15 to 20 seconds. You should have about 4½ cups of sauce; divide the sauce in half and reserve half (about 2¼ cups) for this recipe. (Save the other half for the Cheesy Spinach Stuffed Shells, page 67.)

3 Lay the poblanos on their flattest side on a clean work surface. Use a sharp knife to cut nearly through the top and bottom of each pepper, leaving ½ inch uncut at both the stem and pointed ends. Slit the chiles and open lengthwise, then remove and discard the seeds and white membranes with a small spoon. Brush the insides and outsides of the chiles with 1 tablespoon oil, then season the insides with salt.

4 Grate the mushrooms on the large holes of a box grater; you should have about 1½ cups lightly packed. Grate the carrot on the smaller holes of the grater and add to the mushrooms.

5 Heat the remaining 2 tablespoons oil in a 12-inch skillet over medium heat. Add the onion and cook, stirring until lightly golden, 8 to 9 minutes. Add the garlic, jalapeño, and cumin and cook, stirring, 1 more minute. Transfer the mixture to a large bowl and let cool for 5 minutes. Wash and dry the skillet.

6 Add the grated mushrooms and carrots to the onion mixture, then stir in the cauliflower rice, 1 cup of the cheese blend, the bread crumbs, corn, ½ cup cilantro, and remaining teaspoon salt. Divide the filling evenly among the 4 poblanos (about 1 packed cup in each).

7 Spread the marinara–red pepper sauce in the cleaned skillet and place the stuffed poblanos, cut side up, on top of the sauce. Cover the skillet tightly with aluminum foil and bake until the poblanos soften and the sauce begins to bubble, 30 minutes. Uncover, scatter the remaining ½ cup cheese blend over the poblanos, and bake, uncovered, until the cheese is melted and the sauce thickens slightly, about 8 minutes. Divide the stuffed poblanos and sauce among 4 plates and garnish with the cilantro and cotija.

Fire-Roasted Peppers

To make your own fire-roasted peppers, preheat the oven to 450°F. Place 2 large red bell peppers on a foil-lined baking sheet (standing up, if possible) and roast until puffed and charred on all sides, 30 to 35 minutes. Carefully transfer to a bowl and seal immediately with plastic wrap; let cool completely, at least 1 hour, then uncover, slip the skins off the peppers with your hands, open them up, and remove and discard the seeds. Do not rinse.

CRUMBLE!

desserts

white chocolate
maca-
damia
cookies

MAKES 18 TO 20 COOKIES
ACTIVE TIME: 25 MINUTES
TOTAL TIME: 1 HOUR 40 MINUTES
(INCLUDING MINIMUM CHILLING TIME)

There aren't many things better than a good ol'-fashioned American food court and its crown jewel, Mrs. Fields. When I was a kid, my mom used to be a shopping addict, which is ironic as we didn't have the money then. (Now she barely buys anything.) And when we'd go to the mall, she'd always leave my ass at the Mrs. Fields to let a boxful of these buttery little bundles babysit me.

We've successfully matched that butteriness and somehow, someway created what is TRULY, TRULY, one of the greatest cookies ever made. I'm not kidding. I'm not a crazy cookie lady, but these make me a crazy cookie lady. A kooky lady! Sigh.

Anyhoo, this baby has the three sugars of the gods: light brown sugar, dark brown sugar, and white sugar. Not only does it have all the sugars, but it also has salt. The salt makes this cookie! Also, dough refrigeration is key here. If the dough is too warm, your butter is too warm, and your cookie will spread much too quickly and be more of a cracker in the end. But, hey! As a lover of Tate's, too, maybe you'll experiment and find a butter warmth that fits all your desires. But if you'd like it exactly as *I* personally desire, follow This. Exact. Recipe. You will not need other humans near you for a while.

2½ cups flour

½ teaspoon baking soda

1½ teaspoons fine sea salt

½ cup (lightly packed) light brown sugar

½ cup (lightly packed) dark brown sugar

½ cup granulated sugar

2 sticks (½ pound) cold unsalted butter, cut into small cubes

2 eggs

1 tablespoon vanilla extract

1½ cups white chocolate chunks or chips

1 cup salt-roasted macadamia nut pieces, or toasted, salted pecan pieces

Maldon or other flaky sea salt (or kosher!), for sprinkling

1 In a medium bowl, whisk together the flour, baking soda, and salt.

2 In the bowl of a stand mixer fitted with the paddle attachment, combine the sugars with the butter and beat on medium-high speed until creamy and fluffy, 3 to 4 minutes. Stop the mixer, scrape down the sides of the bowl with a spatula, lower the speed to medium, then add the eggs and vanilla and beat until incorporated, 45 seconds.

3 Reduce the speed to low, then add the flour mixture and beat until just incorporated, 20 to 30 seconds. Add the chocolate and nuts and beat on low speed until just incorporated, a few seconds. Press plastic wrap onto the surface of the dough and chill in the refrigerator for 1 hour.

4 Preheat the oven to 325°F. Lightly coat 2 baking sheets with nonstick cooking spray. Use a cookie scoop (or measuring cup) to measure out ¼ cup portions of dough and space the cookies out on the baking sheets about 4 inches apart from one another. Sprinkle GENEROUSLY with Maldon salt and bake until the edges are browned and the tops are just set but still soft, 14 to 15 minutes. Serve warm.

sour cream blueberry pie

SERVES 8
ACTIVE TIME: 30 MINUTES
TOTAL TIME: 5 HOURS (INCLUDING MINIMUM CHILLING TIME)

My dad has always loved these flavors, so some version of this pie has graced many family gatherings, and my golden teenaged years were marked with individual slices of sour cream blueberry pie from Marie Callender's. But here's the thing: back then, I was also completely grossed out and terrified by the words "sour cream." So now, at age thirty-five, I'd say it's been nineteen extremely wild years.

But Marie Callender's, by the way, changed the name to Double Cream Blueberry Pie, probably because, like me, a lot of people were weirded out by sour cream in a pie. And if that means more for me, then so be it.

I take no issue in saying mine is the best version you'll ever find, with a graham cracker crust, a blueberry-studded custard, and a crumble topping. I could go on and on, but if you're not making it by now, you don't deserve it!! More for me!!

Filling & Pie

1½ cups sour cream

½ teaspoon finely grated orange zest

⅓ cup granulated sugar

⅓ cup light brown sugar

2 eggs

1 teaspoon vanilla extract

¼ teaspoon kosher salt

2½ cups fresh blueberries

1 (9-inch) store-bought graham cracker crust

Topping

½ cup chopped pecans

6 tablespoons light brown sugar

¼ cup flour

3 tablespoons very cold unsalted butter, cut into tiny cubes

¼ teaspoon fine sea salt

Sweet Cream

1 cup heavy cream

3 tablespoons confectioners' sugar

1 MAKE THE FILLING AND BAKE THE PIE: Preheat the oven to 350°F. In a medium bowl, whisk the sour cream, orange zest, sugar, brown sugar, eggs, vanilla, and kosher salt. Stir in the blueberries. Pour the filling into the pie crust, set on a baking sheet and bake until still jiggly but the top feels slightly set, 25 to 40 minutes. Cool the pie completely, then chill at least 3 hours and up to 24 hours.

2 MAKE THE TOPPING: After the pie has cooled, preheat the oven to 350°F again. Combine the pecans, brown sugar, flour, butter, and sea salt in a medium bowl. Pinch with your fingers until most of the mixture resembles giant grains of sand, with some larger buttery clumps. Scatter the topping on a large parchment-lined baking sheet and bake until it is lightly golden and crisp, 15 to 17 minutes.

3 MAKE THE SWEET CREAM AND SERVE: In a large bowl, whisk together the cream and confectioners' sugar until it holds soft peaks. Dollop the cream onto the pie, then sprinkle the topping over the cream. Serve immediately.

HATE LEMON DESSERTS - ORANGE ZEST?

ginger snap
cookie butter

MAKES 1½ CUPS
ACTIVE TIME: 5 MINUTES
TOTAL TIME: 5 MINUTES

The two words that the devil never wanted to go together must be "cookie" and "butter." The phenomenon comes from speculoos, a spiced biscuit popular in Europe. Speculoos then became a *spread*, like peanut butter . . . only it's cookie butter. Literally, it's a spread made from cookies. If you think you've never had speculoos, perhaps you've never been on a Delta flight (Wait . . . do you know I am OBSESSED with airplane food? I've only mentioned it like three times in this book, so I want to make sure you know about it), where one of the (only) best moments is being handed your tiny two-cookie pack of Biscoff cookies, a.k.a. speculoos. And they are a delight.

Here, since we didn't wanna get sued and I also didn't wanna take that many Delta flights to acquire these, we used gingersnaps instead of Biscoff to make our own cookie butter. And, oh baby, did we spiral afterward, thinking of how to use it. We lost our minds. We started stuffing the spread into anything we could find, landing finally, after a long night of experimenting, on a broiled croissant, our cookie butter oozing out the sides. I beg you to find YOUR cookie butter usage, as you'll find yourself using this butter-cookie blended beast to make nearly every dessert or breakfast item better. Pancakes, toast, ice cream, dip for pretzels, stirred into shakes. Or just eaten by the spoonful, like me.

Cookie Butter–Filled Croissants

Split a croissant horizontally like a sandwich bun but leaving one end attached. Spread 2 to 3 tablespoons room-temperature Ginger Snap Cookie Butter inside. Fold the top back over, place on a baking sheet, and bake at 350°F until the top is toasted, 10 to 11 minutes.

½ (8-ounce) package cream cheese, at room temperature

1 stick (8 tablespoons) salted butter (or 1 stick unsalted plus 1 teaspoon kosher salt), at room temperature

¼ cup lightly toasted chopped walnuts

2 tablespoons honey

⅛ teaspoon ground cinnamon

20 ginger snaps (about 5 ounces)

¼ teaspoon kosher salt

Place all the ingredients in a food processor and process until mostly smooth, about 1 minute, stopping occasionally to scrape the sides of the bowl. (The cookie butter will keep in an airtight container in the fridge for up to 2 weeks. Let it come to room temperature before serving.)

sweet & salty family-sized crème brûlée

SERVES 4
ACTIVE TIME: 20 MINUTES
TOTAL TIME: 4 HOURS 35 MINUTES
(INCLUDING MINIMUM CHILLING TIME)

I know. You think the torch is a bit much. You want to turn the page, but pleasssssssssse, I beg you, please stay!! Torches have become extremely popular in the home-cooking world, and there are even TikTok pages dedicated to people delicately torching desserts, getting that thin layer of sugar to turn into sweet, beautiful caramelized glass in one toasty instant. And if you don't wanna torch, you can broil it instead.

And let's talk about the cream. Or the CRÈME, that is. Oh, it is gorgeous. It reminds me of a more upscale version of those childhood vanilla pudding four-packs, with a salty little twist.

This dish is actually painfully easy, the pain being the feeling I get when I know that you think it's harder than it is. Make it once, and I promise you'll see!

1½ cups heavy cream

½ cup half-and-half

¾ cup sugar

5 egg yolks

2 teaspoons vanilla extract

½ teaspoon fine sea salt

1 Preheat the oven to 325°F (if your oven runs hot, set it a drop lower). If you have a kettle for boiling water, fill it and bring it to a boil so you have hot water ready. If not, bring a saucepan of hot water to a boil, then reduce the heat to medium-low to maintain a simmer.

2 Combine the cream and half-and-half in a small saucepan and warm over medium-low heat until just steaming, stirring occasionally and making sure not to bring it to a boil or scorch the mixture.

3 While the cream is warming, combine ½ cup of the sugar and the egg yolks in a medium-large heatproof bowl and whisk until fluffy and pale yellow in color, 1 minute.

4 Remove the warmed cream from the stove, add the vanilla and salt, and whisk it in a slow, steady trickle (at first) into the egg yolk mixture to warm it up (this is called tempering, and it helps you avoid scrambling the eggs). After you've whisked about half the cream into the eggs (the mixture should feel warm), then you can pour the rest in more freely.

5 Pour the mixture into a 1-quart square (about 7-inch) baking dish or oval ramekin (6 × 9-inch) and set it inside a larger, rimmed baking dish. Carefully pour the boiling water into the larger dish to fill it about halfway up the smaller dish. Carefully transfer to the oven and bake until the mixture is just set but still jiggly in the center (the top may be a light golden brown), 30 to 35 minutes.

6 Carefully remove the dishes from the oven, then carefully remove the inner dish from the water and cool at room temperature for 1 hour. Cover with plastic wrap and chill for at least 2 hours and up to 24 hours.

7 When ready to brûlée, sprinkle the remaining ¼ cup sugar evenly over the top of the custard, then use a brûlée torch to caramelize the sugar until it's golden all over, about 2 minutes total. If you don't have a torch, set the oven rack about 4 inches from the broiler and preheat the broiler. Place the dish with the sugar on a baking sheet and place under the broiler until the sugar melts, bubbles, and caramelizes, 3 to 4 minutes. Let stand 5 minutes for the sugar to fully cool and harden before serving.

tres leches

strawberry cakes

MAKES 6 CAKES
ACTIVE TIME: 40 MINUTES
TOTAL TIME: 2 HOURS 40 MINUTES
(INCLUDING MINIMUM CHILLING TIME)

I cannot express how much I love a grocery store. Bristol Farms, the market I simply refuse to live more than 10 minutes away from, is where I get photographed more than any other place in the world. I go four or five times a week, sometimes twice a day. Damn, just writing that made me realize I am bonkers, but oh well!

My point is, do you remember those little grocery store eight-packs of uber-moist yellow cake with the little divot in the center you'd load strawberry goo into? Right? The goo was basically a gel with strawberries floating in it. And God, I how I miss them. I can't find them anywhere! So, I'm bringing them back into my life, and making it homemade-better with an idea inspired by Mexican tres leches cake, which is made by soaking cake in . . . tres leches. (That means "three milks" in Spanish, which . . . you'll figure out why.) Every single layer of this cake is its own delicious little universe of taste. Luna and I love using cookie cutters to theme it up, but a simple biscuit cutter or glass will do. Have fun!

Cake

1¼ sticks (10 tablespoons) unsalted butter, at room temperature, plus more for greasing the pan

1¾ cups flour

1½ teaspoons baking powder

1 teaspoon fine sea salt

1¼ cups granulated sugar

1½ teaspoons vanilla extract

2 eggs

¾ cup whole milk

Strawberry Gel & Garnish

1¾ pounds fresh strawberries, hulled and sliced (about 5 cups)

½ cup granulated sugar

1½ tablespoons cornstarch

1 tablespoon water

1 teaspoon lemon juice

Tres Leches Soak

½ cup heavy cream

½ cup whole milk

½ cup sweetened condensed milk

Whipped Cream

1 cup heavy cream

2 tablespoons confectioners' sugar

RECIPE CONTINUES

1 BAKE THE CAKE: Set a rack in the center of the oven and preheat the oven to 350°F. Grease a small sheet pan (9 × 13-inch) generously with some butter.

2 In a small bowl, whisk together the flour, baking powder, and salt. Melt 5 tablespoons of the butter in the microwave until JUST melted (or very, very soft), 15 to 20 seconds, adding only a few seconds, if necessary.

3 Add the melted butter, the remaining 5 tablespoons of butter, and the sugar to a stand mixer fitted with the paddle attachment and beat on medium-high speed until light and fluffy, 3 minutes, adding the vanilla during the last 15 seconds. Add the eggs, one at a time, beating after each addition and scraping down the sides of the bowl if necessary. Reduce the speed to medium-low and gradually add half the flour mixture, then the milk, then the other half of the flour mixture, beating until just combined after each addition.

4 Transfer the batter to the buttered pan and bake, turning halfway through, until the top is lightly golden, the cake springs back, and a toothpick inserted in the center comes out clean, 19 to 21 minutes. Cool the cake completely in the pan on a wire rack, about 1 hour, then use a 4-inch decorative round cookie cutter or glass to cut out 6 mini-cakes (eat the scraps!).

5 MAKE THE GEL: In a medium saucepan, combine 4 cups of the strawberries with the sugar. In a small bowl, dissolve the cornstarch in the tablespoon water, and add that to the strawberry-sugar mixture. Bring it to a boil over medium heat, stirring often until the sugar melts and the strawberries begin to release their liquid. Reduce the heat to medium-low and simmer, stirring often, until the liquid bubbles, thickens to a jam-like consistency, and glazes the strawberries, about 10 minutes. Stir in the lemon juice, transfer to a bowl, cover with plastic wrap, and cool to room temperature, about 1 hour.

6 MAKE THE TRES LECHES SOAK: In a measuring cup, whisk together the cream, milk, and condensed milk.

7 MAKE THE WHIPPED CREAM: In a large bowl using a whisk or hand mixer, or in a stand mixer, whip together the cream and confectioners' sugar until it holds soft peaks, 2 minutes.

8 Arrange the cutout cakes on a small rimmed baking sheet. Poke holes in the cakes with the narrow end of a chopstick, then soak the cakes with the tres leches mixture; let sit for 10 minutes or until the cream mixture is completely absorbed! Carefully transfer the cakes to serving plates and top each cake with the strawberry gel, then decorate with the whipped cream and the remaining 1 cup sliced fresh strawberries.

apple pie cinnamon buns

with brown butter 'n' booze icing

MAKES 9 ROLLS
ACTIVE TIME: 45 MINUTES
TOTAL TIME: 3 HOURS 15 MINUTES (INCLUDING RISING TIME)

The scene: New Year's weekend. I'm on a boat. (VERY relatable.) I want to make an apple pie, then have an idea to crumble up the pie and fold it into homemade ice cream (ALSO very relatable??). And then I'm, like no, no: it's got to be a warm, buttery cinnamon roll, loaded with caramelly apples and topped with TONS of icing. This has happened to you, I know it.

This all came about because man, oh man, have I gotten into sweets lately: chocolate bars, cheapo maple crullers from Tasty Donuts in L.A., Rice Krispies treats—you name it. But if I'm not in some sort NEEDINMYMOUTHTHISSECOND time crunch, I looooooove a day of baking cinnamon rolls. The process is so soothing to me. Long but simple. The making of the dough, the rise, the rolling, the filling, the rising again, the icing. That right there sounds like a goddamn mantra! Sometimes I even do it over a period of a couple days (you can let the rolled buns sit in the fridge overnight, then do the second rise the next day), just to spread out the joy of making them.

It took me a couple times to perfect all the parts and how they go together, but in the process of getting the butter browned, the tart apples caramelized, and the icing to its boozy best, let's just say even the f*ckups were DEVOURED. So, just imagine how good the *final* version of these puppies, which I give to you here, tastes.

Buns

⅔ cup whole milk

1¾ teaspoons instant, quick rise, or bread machine yeast

3 tablespoons granulated sugar

1 egg, lightly beaten

3 tablespoons unsalted butter, melted

3 cups flour, plus more as needed

¾ teaspoon fine sea salt

Fillings

½ cup (packed) dark brown sugar

1 tablespoon ground cinnamon

¼ teaspoon grated nutmeg

¼ teaspoon fine sea salt

2 medium apples (such as Fuji or Honeycrisp)

1 stick (8 tablespoons) unsalted butter, at room temperature

3 tablespoons granulated sugar

2 tablespoons bourbon

1½ teaspoons cornstarch

1 tablespoon water

Frosting

6 tablespoons (3 ounces) cream cheese, at room temperature

1 cup confectioners' sugar

¼ teaspoon salt

1 tablespoon whole milk

1 tablespoon bourbon

RECIPE CONTINUES

1 MAKE THE BUN DOUGH: Place the milk in a microwave-safe mug and microwave on high until warm (about 110°F), 30 to 35 seconds. (Use a thermometer or your finger; it should feel like really warm bath water, but not scalding hot.) Add the milk to the bowl of a stand mixer and scatter the yeast on top, then add the sugar, egg, and melted butter. Attach the dough hook, and mix on low speed until the ingredients begin to unify, 15 seconds. Increase the speed to medium-low, gradually add the flour, and mix the dough for 3 minutes, then add the salt. Continue to mix until the dough is slightly tacky but pulls away from the sides and bottom of the mixer, about 5 minutes. Lightly grease a medium bowl, transfer the dough to the bowl, seal with plastic wrap, and let rise in a warm place until doubled in size, 1 hour 15 minutes.

2 WHILE THE DOUGH IS RISING, MAKE THE FILLINGS: In a small bowl, combine the brown sugar, 2 teaspoons of the cinnamon, the nutmeg, and 1/8 teaspoon salt in a small bowl.

3 Peel, core, and halve the apples. Cut each apple half into 8 wedges, then cut the wedges crosswise into thin slices. Heat 5 tablespoons of the butter in a 9- or 10-inch skillet over medium-high heat, stirring often, until foamy and toasty with brown flecks, 4 minutes. Scoop out 2 tablespoons of the browned butter and place in a small heatproof bowl, then set aside for the frosting. To the skillet, add the sliced apples, sugar, bourbon, remaining teaspoon cinnamon,

and remaining 1/8 teaspoon salt and cook, shaking and stirring occasionally, until the liquid begins to thicken, 2 minutes. Cover, reduce the heat to medium-low, and simmer until the apples soften and turn golden, 4 to 5 minutes, stirring once midway through.

4 In a small bowl, stir together the cornstarch with the tablespoon water. Uncover the pan, then stir in the dissolved cornstarch and cook, stirring constantly, until the liquid thickens, about 1 minute. Transfer the apple mixture to a plate to cool to room temperature.

5 FILL AND FORM THE BUNS: Line the bottom and sides of a 9- or 10-inch round or square baking pan with parchment paper. Once the dough has risen, lightly flour a work surface and turn the dough out onto the surface.

6 Gently shape the dough into a rectangle, then roll out into a 9 × 13-inch rectangle. Spread the remaining 3 tablespoons room temperature butter over the dough, then sprinkle and press the brown sugar mixture into the butter. Spoon the cooled apple mixture evenly over the sugar, pressing gently. Starting from one of the short ends, roll the dough into a tight log, trying to pull the sides of the dough out as you go to keep the roll uniform.

7 Trim 1/2 inch off each end, then use a ruler to mark the roll evenly into 9 pieces (each about 1 inch thick). Dust a serrated knife with a little flour and gently saw through the dough to create 9 rolls. Carefully separate the rolls (some apple filling might try

to escape, keep it in line!) and fit them into the pan. Seal with plastic wrap and let rise again until puffy, about 45 minutes.

8 Preheat the oven to 350°F. Remove the plastic wrap and bake the rolls until fluffy and golden on top, about 25 minutes.

9 WHILE THE ROLLS ARE BAKING, MAKE THE FROSTING: In the bowl of an electric mixer fitted with the paddle attachment, combine the cream cheese, reserved 2 tablespoons browned butter, confectioners' sugar, and salt and beat on low speed for 30 seconds. Increase the speed to high, beat 30 seconds, then add the milk and bourbon and beat until fluffy and light, 2 to 3 minutes.

10 Remove the rolls from the oven, let cool 5 minutes, then spread the frosting on the rolls!

vanilla sheet cake

with salted milk chocolate frosting

SERVES 16
ACTIVE TIME: 20 MINUTES
TOTAL TIME: 2 HOURS 15 MINUTES
(INCLUDING MINIMUM COOLING TIME)

Glued into my memory is the kind of lazy cake that I now *completely* understand as a busy parent. If you have the time to bake several cakes, make fillings and frostings, and construct them like a house of dreams, go for it. If you don't . . . you throw batter in a sheet pan and boom: cake.

My favorite combo was always the bright yellow "vanilla" cake with chocolate frosting and the cheapest, most flavorless sprinkles possible. Here, I've used milk chocolate for the frosting to avoid any sort of dark bitterness (admitted non-chocoholic), and the cream cheese adds to the tang. Adeena (the most badass co-author I could ever ask for) made the comment that the cream cheese also ensures you get that neat little tooth mark in the frosting after each bite. And you know when frosting has that "coolness" to it? Not the hip type of cool but actual cold, chocolatey chilliness when it hits your tongue? It's weird, but it speaks to me. Immediately after mixing, I use a butter knife to gently swipe frosting across my entire tongue, achieving maximum icy coolness.

Cake

2 sticks (½ pound) unsalted butter, at room temperature, plus more for the baking pan

2 cups flour

1½ teaspoons baking powder

1½ teaspoons fine sea salt

2 cups granulated sugar

3 eggs, plus 1 egg yolk

¾ cup sour cream

1½ tablespoons vanilla extract

Frosting

1¼ cups milk chocolate chips

½ (8-ounce) package cream cheese, cold

3 tablespoons unsalted butter, at room temperature

1 teaspoon vanilla extract

½ teaspoon fine sea salt, or more if you're a salt hound

2¾ cups sifted confectioners' sugar

Sprinkles of your choice

1 MAKE THE CAKE: Preheat the oven to 350°F. Generously butter a 9 × 13-inch baking pan.

2 Whisk together the flour, baking powder, and salt in a bowl. Beat the 2 sticks of butter and the sugar in a stand mixer fitted with the paddle attachment over medium-high speed until the color lightens and the mix is fluffy, 2 to 3 minutes. Add the eggs and egg yolk and beat, scraping down the sides of the bowl if necessary, until just combined. Reduce the speed to medium-low and add half the flour mixture, then half the sour cream, then the remaining flour and then the remaining sour cream. Add the vanilla at the end, mixing only until all is just combined.

3 Spoon the batter into the prepared pan, spread into an even layer, and bake until the top is lightly browned, the cake is just completely set, and a toothpick inserted comes out clean, 35 to 40 minutes. Remove from the oven and cool completely on a wire rack, about 1 hour.

4 MAKE THE FROSTING: Place the chocolate chips in a microwave-safe bowl and heat on high until just fully melted, stopping every 30 seconds to stir, 60 to 90 seconds total (the more you melt the chocolate, the longer you're going to have to let it cool). Let the chocolate cool to room temperature, about 20 minutes (the outside of the bowl should feel just slightly warm or not warm at all).

5 Scrape the melted chocolate into the bowl of a stand mixer fitted with the paddle attachment, then add the cream cheese, butter, vanilla, and salt and beat at high speed until incorporated and slightly fluffy, stopping and scraping down the sides of the bowl if necessary, 1 minute. Reduce the speed to low, then slowly add the confectioners' sugar. Beat until it's no longer dusty and powdery. Raise the speed to high and beat until light and fluffy, 2 to 3 minutes.

6 Spread the frosting across the cooled cake, top with the sprinkles, and cut into squares to serve.

peanut butter & potato chip

seven-layer bars

MAKES 24 BARS
ACTIVE TIME: 15 MINUTES
TOTAL TIME: 2 HOURS (INCLUDING MINIMUM COOLING TIME)

The idea with these kinds of bars is that one layer sinks into the other until all the flavors meld, but I wanted something crunchy and salty to contrast with all the sweetness here. They're often made with butterscotch chips, but a certain EGOT loves his peanut butter, so I went ahead and did him a solid here (and did myself one by using milk chocolate, which—sorry, chocosnobs—will always be my favorite). For the potato chips, use really thin, classic goes-with-your-sandwich chips (rhymes with "braise"), which crush up into lovely little shards and almost melt in your mouth, like crushed potato frosting.

7 tablespoons unsalted butter, melted

30 Oreo cookies

¼ teaspoon fine sea salt

1¼ cups peanut butter chips

1¼ cups milk chocolate chips

1½ cups chopped salted walnuts*

1 (14-ounce) can sweetened condensed milk

1½ cups sweetened shredded coconut

2 cups thin, classic potato chips (we like Lay's), crushed but not pulverized (1 cup crushed)

*If you don't have salted walnuts, toss 1½ cups chopped unsalted walnuts with 1 teaspoon vegetable oil and ¼ teaspoon fine sea salt.

1 Preheat the oven to 350°F. Use 1 tablespoon of the melted butter to coat the bottom and sides of a 9 × 13-inch baking pan.

2 Place the cookies in a food processor and process until fine crumbs form, 15 to 20 seconds. Stop the processor, add the remaining 6 tablespoons melted butter and the salt, and pulse until incorporated, about 10 pulses.

3 Press the cookie mixture into the bottom of the baking pan. Sprinkle the peanut butter chips and chocolate chips evenly over the surface, then sprinkle the nuts evenly over the chips. Drizzle all but 2 tablespoons of the condensed milk over the nuts. In a bowl, toss together the coconut and potato chips, sprinkle evenly over the top, then drizzle the remaining 2 tablespoons condensed milk over all to help the chips stick.

4 Bake until the sides are bubbling and the coconut and chips are golden, 25 minutes. Cool completely (at least 1½ hours), then cut into 24 squares.

frosted circus animal cookies

MAKES 100 (1 × 2-INCH) COOKIES
ACTIVE TIME: 1 HOUR 15 MINUTES
TOTAL TIME: 3 HOURS 15 MINUTES
(INCLUDING MINIMUM CHILLING TIME)

I discovered the most adorable animal cookie cutters in the world, and they make me just want to make cookies all the time. I also have two cookie monsters in my home, so it works out. These are like the cookies you got in the pink and white bag when you were a kid, except with a little more grownup flavor in the actual cookie itself, thanks to a nice little warm spice blend of cinnamon and nutmeg.

The white chocolate covering keeps them classically sweet, the sprinkles are for the kiddies, and the salt is for me (and you). I know that cutting and frosting 100 cookies seems like a *lot*, but when you see how easy it is to eat 20 in one sitting, you'll get it. You can halve the recipe, too, if for whatever reason having 100 cookies isn't your vibe.

2 sticks (½ pound) unsalted butter, at room temperature

⅔ cup sugar

1 teaspoon vanilla extract

2⅓ cups flour*

½ teaspoon fine sea salt

⅛ teaspoon ground cinnamon

⅛ teaspoon grated nutmeg

1 (12-ounce) bag Brilliant White Candy Melts (that's their name) or other white chocolate chips

2 tablespoons canola or vegetable oil, plus more as needed

Pink food coloring

3 tablespoons tiny multicolored nonpareil sprinkles

*If halving the recipe, reduce all ingredients by half; use 1 cup plus 3 tablespoons flour.

1 In a stand mixer fitted with the paddle attachment, beat the butter, sugar, and vanilla on medium speed until well combined, 30 to 45 seconds. Reduce the speed to low and gradually add the flour, salt, cinnamon, and nutmeg, beating until the dough just starts to clump together, about 45 seconds.

2 Divide the dough into 2 balls, then place each ball on a large piece of parchment, flatten into a disc, and cover with another piece of parchment. Roll each disc of dough to a ¼-inch thickness. Place the 2 parchment-sandwiched dough sheets on a baking sheet and chill in the fridge for at least 1 hour and up to 24 hours.

3 Preheat the oven to 300°F. Remove the dough from the fridge, uncover, use small (about 1 × 2-inch) animal cookie cutters to cut into animal shapes, and carefully transfer them to parchment-lined baking sheets (use an offset spatula if you have one), spacing the cookies at least ½ inch apart. Reroll the dough scraps and rechill until firm (about 30 minutes) to make more cookies.

4 Bake until the cookies are pale golden and some of the edges have slightly darkened, 11 to 12 minutes. (The coating softens the cookies slightly, so don't be tempted to underbake.) Cool completely on baking sheets set on a wire rack, about 30 minutes.

5 **FOR DECORATING:** Make room in the fridge for a large baking sheet. Line the baking sheet with wax or parchment paper. Divide the melts into 2 medium microwave-safe bowls (1 cup each) and add 1 tablespoon oil to each bowl. Microwave one bowl of melts in 30-second increments until melty and liquidy (about 1½ minutes total), making sure not to overheat as the chocolate will begin to seize. The chocolate won't be runny, but it will be dippable; stir in ½ teaspoon oil at a time if the chocolate is too thick.

6 Use a fork to dip the top side of 30 cookies into the melted chocolate, then tap the dipped cookies against the edge of the bowl to drip extra chocolate off the cookie. Arrange the cookies, frosting side up, on the lined baking sheet and sprinkle with the nonpareils before the chocolate dries.

7 Melt the rest of the melts using the same method, then add food coloring to achieve the desired shade of pink (2 or 3 drops). Repeat the dipping and sprinkling, then place the cookies in the fridge until they are hard to the touch, 20 to 30 minutes. (Store the cookies in an airtight container at room temperature for up to 3 days.)

unicorn milk-shakes

MAKES 2 SHAKES
ACTIVE TIME: 20 MINUTES
TOTAL TIME: 20 MINUTES

UGGGGHHHHHHHH, this is so good that you can truly just let your kids have a sip (they'll be SO happy) and take the rest to drink with you to go cry in the closet over the state of the world. (I figure this thought is evergreen now, so I've decided to just go ahead and write this in my book.)

Anyhoo, these shakes are the opposite of sad: they are pudding-powder milkshake cups of unicorn magic, with random crunches of sugar throughout, topped with flavored cream and more sprinkles. They shoot instant happiness into both your heart and brain. If you're making them for young kids, just trust me when I say they'll f*cking love it. And you will, too: Luna had two sips and went into a birthday-party-sugar-coma six-hour sleep so youuuuuuu are welcome.

4 cups whole milk (or alternative milk of your choice)

1 (3.4-ounce) package instant vanilla pudding mix (make sure it's instant!)

Pinch of kosher salt

Assorted colors of fine sanding sugar

1 cup heavy cream

2 tablespoons confectioners' sugar

2 tablespoons corn syrup

Special Equipment

Small pastry brush or other clean paint brush, preferably no more than ½ inch wide

Whipped cream dispenser (totally optional!)*

1 In a pitcher or other pourable container, whisk together the milk, pudding mix, and salt and refrigerate until ready to use (up to 3 days in advance).

2 In a medium bowl, dissolve 1 teaspoon of the sanding sugar color of your choice (Luna likes pink!) in a few drops of hot water and whisk it with the cream and confectioners' sugar. If using the whipped cream canister, pour it into the canister and chill. Otherwise, whip it by hand to soft peaks and refrigerate. (If you've never done this before, just whip the cream with a whisk and you'll see it eventually thicken. When it gets thick enough to hold little peaks that flop over at the tip of the whisk, you're done.)

3 Select the right glass—something between 12 and 16 ounces, something you would want to drink a shake out of—made of clear glass is good! Or use coffeehouse-style to-go plastic cups with domed tops). Set up as many small pinch bowls as you have colors of sanding sugar.

4 Dip the end of the pastry brush into the corn syrup (less is more here) and, starting from the inside base of the glass, paint a strip of corn syrup up to the top of the glass. Sprinkle the first color of sanding sugar on top of the corn syrup, shaking and tapping to cover. Turn the excess sanding sugar back out into its pinch bowl. Continue with the corn syrup and sanding sugar, until the entire inside of the glass is colored. Fill the glass with 1½ cups of the vanilla pudding shake, then top with a generous amount of colored whipped cream. Sprinkle the cream with sanding sugar to decorate and place a colorful straw in the shake.

Get Fancy

Using a professional whipped cream dispenser will get you fancy cream and make you feel like a chef. They're as cheap as $30, and a box of 24 "chargers"—basically, whippets—will run you about $25. Every time you want to make fresh whipped cream you pour it into the dispenser, then use a charger to infuse the cream with CO_2.

crispy-chewy
pop-corn balls

MAKES 9 BALLS
ACTIVE TIME: 25 MINUTES
TOTAL TIME: 25 MINUTES

These came about after a conversation with friends about the "good houses" on Halloween, the ones with full-sized candy bars, candy apples, and popcorn balls. I couldn't stop thinking about the popcorn balls! Back before salty-sweet was A THING, there they were. Anyway, then I remembered an earlier convo I had with Adeena about wanting to re-create those Golden Grahams cereal bars from back in the day that my mom thought were granola bars—i.e., *healthy*—and we were off to the races.

These ooooooooze fall, with their pops of graham goodness. The real magic is in the marshmallow (two kinds!), with a near-appalling amount of butter mixed into the sticky goo, and I have ZERO apologies for it.*

1 stick (8 tablespoons) salted butter

1 (12-ounce) bag large marshmallows

2 tablespoons corn syrup

½ teaspoon kosher salt

6 cups lightly salted popped popcorn

2 cups Rice Krispies cereal

1½ cups Golden Grahams cereal

1 cup mini marshmallows

1 Line a baking sheet with wax paper. Melt the butter in a large (at least 6-quart) pot over medium heat. Add the large marshmallows and cook, stirring, until melted, 3 to 4 minutes. Stir in the corn syrup and salt and cook 1 more minute.

2 Place the popcorn, Rice Krispies, and Golden Grahams in a large bowl. Pour the melted marshmallow mixture over the dry ingredients and stir until everything is coated, trying not to crush the popcorn and cereal, and cool for 2 minutes. Gently stir in the mini marshmallows.

3 Lightly oil or spray your hands with a neutral cooking spray. Use your hands to form about 1 cup of the mixture into a compact but not smashed-together ball. Repeat with the remaining mixture. Wrap individually in cellophane and tie with ribbons.

*To adultify these, add in ½ cup chopped smokehouse almonds or dark chocolate chips!

incredibly easy adorable mini zebra cakes

MAKES 12 MINI CAKES
ACTIVE TIME: 20 MINUTES
TOTAL TIME: 4 HOURS 20 MINUTES
(INCLUDING MINIMUM COOLING TIME)

Remember that TV show *Zoom*? It was sort of the kids' show for the 'N Sync generation. Anyway, in it, they had this short cooking segment when kids would teach kids (me, at the time) how to make something small, tasty, and cute AF.

One little recipe from that show carved out a permanent place in my memory even all these years later: the zebra cake, a magical "cake" of chocolate cookies sandwiched with whipped cream all night until you get this delightful little soft cookies-and-cream dream. The recipe is no secret; the Nabisco chocolate wafer box (and you *do* have to use these, but thankfully every single supermarket on earth carries them in their bright yellow sleeve) has a picture of it on the box. The *Zoom* kids made a single, larger log version, but my household goes bonkers for these little individual yummies. (Ew, I HATE how I talk in these kids' recipes, but it's yum, okay?!?!!)

1 (8-ounce) container Cool Whip, thawed in the fridge overnight

36 Nabisco chocolate wafer cookies

24 small eyeball candies (the cute googly-eye kind, not the gross bloody ones—or you do you)

Chocolate jimmies, for sprinkling

12 (8½-inch) black licorice sticks or chocolate-covered Pocky

1 Transfer the Cool Whip to a large zippered plastic bag and cut a ½-inch hole in one corner. Pipe about 2 tablespoons Cool Whip in a mound onto the center of one cookie. Sandwich with a second cookie and gently press down until the Cool Whip squeezes to the edge and the filling layer is about ½ inch thick.

2 Repeat the process with another 2 tablespoons Cool Whip and a third cookie to form a 3-layer stack. Transfer the cookie stack to a parchment-lined baking sheet. Repeat with the remaining cookies and Cool Whip to form 12 total stacks, reserving about 1 tablespoon of Cool Whip. Attach 2 eyes to the top of each stack using the reserved Cool Whip as glue. Chill, uncovered, until the cookies have softened, at least 4 hours or up to overnight.

3 Working with one stack at a time, and holding it over a small rimmed baking sheet, sprinkle the sides of the stack with chocolate jimmies. Repeat with the remaining stacks.

4 Cut each licorice stick or Pocky into 8 even pieces (about 1 inch long). Press 8 pieces into the bottom layer of each stack to resemble legs. Serve immediately or chill for up to 8 hours.

acknowledgments

First, to my incredible, hilarious and talented photo team. Alex, I hesitate to say how great you are in fear others will take you away from me! Emmy + Colby, you guys look like the it couple from *The O.C.* Thank you for being so effortlessly chill amidst my chaos. Kieran, we met for a day and it was glorious, but I know you did so much more behind the scenes, so thank you. Shauna, bless you for figuring out all the different Covid rules to make sure we could have this shoot! Tyna + Scotty, you are the best. I trust you with my life! (Missing Scott's secret moustache. Who knew?!) Sophie + Jaclyn—your eyeballs are nothing short of incredible. Thank you for bringing so much joy and color to this book. Paris, we never could have imagined needing a Covid officer but were lucky to be blessed with you!

My glam team and so much more, you guys are my heart, my family. You have seen everything, wiped away the tears, and replaced them with smiles, physically and mentally. Kristine, Irinel, Alana, Nova: I am so fortunate to have found you in this sea of clutter. My sisters, my girls forever. I am so lucky. I will cry now!

As usual, the beauties who make this shit happen, David Levin + Melissa Konstantatos. David, you silver fox, we trust you and Melissa with all our silver (and gold)! Lily Tillers. We love you. My goodness, you are smarter than I am, and thank God for you!

Luke + Meghan—our best friends who happened to have fallen in love, who also happen to be *crucial* in making my world go round. My biggest cheerleaders, the ones who are the most proud even when I can't feel it. I love you, I'm so lucky to have you both. Hi, Charlotte!

Strand, probably the main reason I have any monies, lol. Your dedication to me and Cravings makes me burst with joy. Every time I see you, I wish we went to college together to party, lol, but alas now we are old!

Erin—I'm already ready for book #4. Are you?? Thank you for trusting me and being so supportive, which paved the way for the PERFECT book.

Marisa—you created this monster! I love you. Thank you for your protection, your friendship, your humor, your guidance. I just love you.

Shim! My true other half, the one who keeps this whole ship afloat. The hardest-working person I know, who can still pause at any moment to lie on the floor with my kids. I forever love you for how you treat my family. You *are* family, whether you like it or not. No pressure, but if I ever lose you I will probably crumble and die. Seriously.

Francis, the man to believe in me from JUMP! My love and admiration for you knows no bounds. Seeing you climb so high in this silly world makes my heart happy.

Stephanie + Marysarah, for your overnight Zooming, attention to detail, and helping design a book that looks exactly how I feel! And thank you, Lydia, for making it *all* easier.

Paige, Ian + Renae—You took these recipes through their paces, and each and every one is better for it. Thank you for your thoughtful and enthusiastic testing!

Adeena. My Adeena! There really isn't anyone else who knows and sees what you've known and seen, lol. What a year, what a journey, just another insane chapter in our long book that is our life together. Always the one with the best advice, best words, best energy. Everyone needs an Adeena. I am *so* glad I have the OG. I'm so proud of you and your cookbook journey! Thank you for ALL you've taught me. Truly one of my best friends, I admire you with all my heart.

Dipple, you video dream! Sorry my daughter always takes your hat. Thank you for seamlessly integrating your camera into our family.

Beezoo, thank you for the bomb-ass catering! Those breakfast sandwiches forever have my heart.

Lorelei, Jasmine, Connie, Josie, Ebony, Allison + Bronwyn—the rocks that hold our family together. We cannot flourish without you. Thank you for cradling me, loving me, holding me through an incredibly hard year. Your love keeps me together.

Finally, my family: Mom + Dad—Thank you for making me, for shaping me into what I am today. All I want is to take care of you forever and make you proud.

Tina, my literal sister, thank you for giving me my daughter's best friend. Thank you for always having a copy of my birth certificate, and for always taking care of me and everyone around you. You are legit a better cook than I am, lol.

Luna + Miles, thank you for giving me a reason to wake up. You both are getting so big and your hearts are growing even faster. I am so proud of what Daddy and I have created. Our little minis! Love you to the moon and back.

My John: It has been a year, hasn't it? Thank you for holding me through it all, for anchoring our family, for keeping it *all together* when I couldn't. My soulmate, my partner for life. Together until the absolute end. I pray I go first—I cannot live without you, my absolute everything.

index